Dracula

Dracula

The ORIGINS *and* INFLUENCE *of* *the* LEGENDARY VAMPIRE COUNT

GILES MORGAN

Oldcastle Books

First published in 2022
by Oldcastle Books, Harpenden, UK
oldcastlebooks.co.uk

Editor: Nick Rennison

A CIP catalogue record for this book is available from the British Library.

ISBN
978-0-85730-443-8 (print)
978-0-85730-444-5 (epub)

2 4 6 8 10 9 7 5 3 1

Typeset in 13 on 16.5pt Adobe Garamond Pro
by Avocet Typeset, Bideford, Devon, EX39 2BP
Printed and bound in Great Britain by Clays Ltd, Elcograf S.p.A.

For Georgina

Contents

Dracula

Introduction

Introduction

When Bram Stoker's *Dracula* was first published in 1897 a legend was born.

Or perhaps more appropriately a legend was reborn as belief in the existence of vampires can be traced far back into the distant past. Stoker's vampiric count is very much a product of the historical period that he was created in and offers a fascinating window on the concerns and neuroses of Victorian society.

However, vampires in the past were conceived to be very different to the rather elegant and strangely attractive aristocrat of Stoker's novel. Early variations of the vampire legend include the figure of Empusa who, in Greek mythology, is the demonic daughter of the goddess Hecate. According to ancient sources Empusa was able to change her shape into the form of a beautiful young woman who seduced unwitting men in order to drink their blood. Further east in Persia, similar stories were told of terrifying creatures that hunger for the blood of men. It is said that the myths concerning the female demon of Jewish culture called Lilith who attacks both men and women were in part influenced by Babylonian tales of a similar figure called Lilitu who, horrifically, drank the blood of babies. The Indian goddess Kali was depicted as having fangs and was believed to drink blood.

Vampires can be found in folklore around the world, from the Jiang Shi of Chinese origin, said to attack people in order to drain them of their life force to the bizarre chupacabra or 'goat-sucker', supposed to exist in the modern era in countries such as Mexico and Puerto Rico. Interestingly, it is arguable that, in Western Europe, Christianity was to play a major role in the popular folk belief in vampires. Indeed Pope Innocent VIII lent weight and credence to the belief in demons and blood-feeding incubi when he published the papal bull *Summis desiderantes affectibus* on 5 December 1484 that acknowledged their existence. Belief in the reality of vampires was particularly intense in the Balkans and throughout Eastern Europe it was believed that, on the eve of certain Christian festivals such as St George's Day, demonic forces grew particularly powerful and that precautions had to be taken against them.

There has been a great deal of speculation about the inspiration behind the creation of Bram Stoker's fictional Count Dracula. Perhaps unsurprisingly many have argued that Stoker derived elements of the count's persona from individuals that he knew. Today Stoker is famous as an author but in his own lifetime he was perhaps better known as the business manager of the Lyceum Theatre and the personal assistant of the actor Sir Henry Irving.

In Victorian society Irving was a hugely popular and famous figure and it has been claimed that Stoker based the character of Dracula, in part at least, on him.

It is known that Stoker spent around seven years researching the subject of vampires in European folklore. Although Stoker took the name Dracula from a medieval Romanian prince better known to history as Vlad the Impaler or Vlad III Dracula there has been some argument over to what extent he based his character on him.

The name Dracula derives from the term 'draco' which in Vlad's time meant dragon but has come to be more specifically seen in later interpretations of the phrase as meaning 'devil'.

Analysis of the known facts about the life of Vlad the Impaler and its influence on Stoker's creation shows interesting parallels between the two not least in physical descriptions that survive of Vlad the Impaler and Stoker's depiction of the fictional count.

But Stoker was also strongly influenced by more recent European literature and in particular the 1819 novella, *The Vampyre*, written by John Polidori. Polidori was the personal physician of the infamous poet Lord Byron whose own colourful life had shocked and outraged many in European society. It is thought that Polidori based his central character on Lord Byron and established the popular idea of the vampire as an aristocratic figure with sensual leanings.

More recently modern critics have come to see Stoker's novel as a fascinating insight into the Victorian mind and its obsessions with death, disease and sexuality as well as offering an interesting metaphor for the emergence of a scientific world of rationalism pitted against a disappearing past based on superstition and fear. The figure of Dracula has, of course, gained greatest prominence and fame within popular culture through the medium of film. There has been a multitude of movies either adapted from or influenced by Stoker's novel including the 1922 German silent film *Nosferatu* and the 1931 Universal horror classic starring Bela Lugosi as the undead count.

The success of the Dracula story has been such that it has filtered into seemingly all levels of popular culture ranging from literary criticism to 1970s exploitation films such as *Blacula*. He has even become an icon of children's entertainment appearing in the television programme *Sesame Street* as the much-loved character of 'The Count', who was based on Bela Lugosi's interpretation of Dracula.

In the 1990s, Francis Ford Coppola produced his version of the original novel called *Bram Stoker's Dracula* and the subject of vampirism has, if anything, grown in popularity and appeal. *Dracula* has also continued to inspire within the literary world and the bestselling novel *The Historian* by Elizabeth Kostova is heavily influenced by Stoker's creation and features the count as its central character.

Most recently writers Mark Gatiss and Steven Moffat have produced a radically different interpretation of *Dracula* in a 2020 BBC television series that features a strong female central character and reconsiders the very nature of the count himself.

It has been suggested that the figure of Dracula has an even greater relevance to the modern world and for the foreseeable future the character shows no signs of resting peacefully in its grave. The legend of the vampire lives on.

Chapter One

The Vampire in European Folklore

Vampires are mythological creatures of folklore and legend that can be found in a wide variety of world cultures. They are conceived of as some form of revenant who has died as a religious heretic or was some other form of social outcast or criminal and they are popularly believed to leave their graves at night to feed on the blood of the living. Commonly, they are said to prey on the communities to which they used to belong. The modern concept of the vampire has, of course, been hugely influenced by Bram Stoker's fictional, aristocratic villain, Count Dracula. The image of the vampire as a frightening yet often attractive and elegant figure has become something of an archetype and can be found in a range of fiction, particularly in the mediums of film and television.

The development of the popular concept of the vampire through literature and cinema will be examined more thoroughly in later chapters but it is important in examining the genesis, production of and influence of *Dracula* to look at the earliest mythological and historical precedents for his character. Whilst modern vampires are imagined as pale and gaunt in appearance, in ancient cultures they were often described as ruddy and swollen from gorging on blood. As we shall see the modern image of the vampire developed mainly in the post-Romantic period and is often markedly different from the brutish, animalistic vampires of myth. Today, of course, vampires are seen as a staple of the horror genre and are seen as products of the superstitious and irrational beliefs of the past. It has been argued that belief in vampires may have developed from fears surrounding death and instances when the bodies of the deceased appeared either not to have decomposed due to the circumstances of their burial or seemed bloated and distended. The continued growth of human hair and nails after death might also lend the appearance of unnatural life to a human corpse. However, as we shall see, belief in real vampires persists to this day with a prime example being the South American chupacabra that is believed to terrorise farm animals and feed on their blood.

The term vampire derives from the early eighteenth century and can be traced mainly to the cultures and superstitions of Eastern Europe. It is a word that can be found in most Slavic languages as 'vampir'. Some have argued that it has made its way into the English language through the German language that also uses the word 'vampir'.

Very often in post-*Dracula* fiction vampires are imagined as sexually threatening male characters but it is interesting to discover that in ancient mythology vampiric beings were often imagined as female and were sexually predatory in nature.

Lilith

It is arguable that the female demon of Jewish culture called Lilith has been one of the greatest influences on the development of the concept of vampires. The origins of Lilith appear to be very ancient, as references can be found to her in the form of a storm demon in ancient Sumerian culture. In this context she was known as Lilitu and belief in her role as a form of wind or storm demon is thought to date to as early as 4000 BC. In the Hebrew Bible Lilith is described in the *Book of Isaiah* 34:14 as residing in the desert. In the fifth-century Vulgate version of *Isaiah* the name Lilith is substituted for the Greek term 'Lamia' which, as we shall see, has similarly vampiric overtones. In the King James Bible (begun in 1604 and completed in 1611), 'Lamia' is re-translated as 'screech-owl'. In Roman mythology the screech-owl is often associated with vampire-like creatures known as the Strix. The motivation for using the term screech-owl may have been that it was difficult to translate the Jewish and Greek terms successfully into English and so they were equated with this night-time bird. Ancient folk traditions record the story that Lilith was the first wife of Adam but refused to submit to him because she was made from the same clay as him.

Lamia

One of the oldest figures from European mythology to share characteristics with the modern concept of the vampire is the female demon Lamia. According to Greek mythology Lamia was the Queen of Libya and came to be seen as a personification of that country. In some versions, she was the daughter of Poseidon the God of the sea and Lybie. As is so often the case in Greek myth, Zeus, the most senior of the Olympian gods, desired Lamia and had an affair with her. She gave birth to several children by him. When Zeus's wife, Hera, discovered this, she was so angry she killed all but one, a child called Scylla. Lamia's pain and grief were so intense at the loss of her children that she began killing children in a twisted form of revenge. Some accounts of this disturbing tale describe Zeus attempting to assuage her loss by granting her the gift of prophecy and by giving her the bizarre ability to pluck out her own eyes and then replace them. She is also described as having a terrifying face and being half human and half snake. It was also said that Lamia would seduce young men and then gorge on their blood whilst they were asleep.

Robert Graves argues that Lamia was the demonised form of the Libyan goddess of War and Love, Neith. The name 'Lamia' seems to derive from the Greek word for gullet which is 'Laimos', an allusion to her eating children. Over time Lamia became a kind of bogeyman figure that Greek mothers would use to frighten their children in order to make them behave. In the *Book of Isaiah* (34: 14), as we have seen, there is a reference to Lilith that Jerome translated in the Vulgate as 'Lamia' and this had the effect of identifying her with the seduction of men just as Lilith had seduced Adam. Lamia was to prove a source of inspiration to a number of later artists such as the painter John William Waterhouse and John Keats who wrote the poem *Lamia* in 1819.

Empusa

In ancient Greek mythology a shape-shifting female being called the Empusa (or Empousa) displays distinctly vampire-like characteristics. They were said to be demons who were the children of the goddess Hecate. In stories about them they are described as having only one leg which is sometimes said to be made of copper and sometimes that of a donkey. Such folklore stated that these beings commonly adopted the form of female animals or beautiful women. When they changed their shape into attractive women they would seduce men and afterwards drain them of their life-force whilst they slept. Interestingly, they were also said to 'frighten travellers, but they may be routed by insulting words, at the sound of which they fly shrieking' (Robert Graves, The Greek Myths, p.189).

It is thought that belief in these beings was probably based on the idea of the children of the demon goddess Lilith who were termed the 'Lilim'. The story was then carried from Palestine to Greece where it was adopted and adapted. The Lilim, like the Greek Empusa, were described in Jewish folklore as 'ass-haunched'. This odd characteristic is believed to derive from the concept of the donkey as a symbol of cruelty and lechery.

Greek Vampires

In later Greek folklore the vrykolakas is said to be a malevolent undead creature that troubles the living. It originates from a Slavic term that commonly was used to describe a werewolf. In other European countries such as Serbia, Croatia and Bosnia the related term 'vukodlak' is now used to mean vampire. As we shall see in Chapter Two the concepts of the vampire and the werewolf are in many ways interlinked.

However the Greek vrykolakas, although similar in many respects to the vampire described in the folklore of the Balkans, is less often described as drinking the blood of its victims. There were believed to be a number of reasons why an individual could become a vrykolakas after their death, many of which can be viewed as punishment for not adhering to Christian values. For example, if a person had been excommunicated by the church and died they could suffer this condition or if they had been buried improperly. It was claimed that a vrykolakas, like the vampire, would not rot in the grave but that their body would remain fresh although it would develop a ruddy appearance.

It was believed that after death the vrykolakas would clamber from its burial site and harass the living by knocking on their doors and shouting out the names of people. It was said that if a person answered the knock at the door or the call of the vrykolakas they would die shortly afterwards. Just as disturbingly it was also thought that the vrykolakas were responsible for the suffocation or crushing of victims during sleep. This is a similar concept to that of the incubus. It was believed that unless the vrykolakas was destroyed it would continue to terrorise the living and was also a plague carrier. It was also thought that the vrykolakas should be destroyed by a combination of impaling the body and severing the head. Afterwards the body was burned.

There is an acknowledgement in stories concerning these undead people that they are not only a threat to living people but that they themselves are trapped in a kind of eternal suffering. This has become a common idea within the mythology surrounding the vampire. During the seventeenth century written accounts of folklore surrounding the vrykolakas began to appear in Western Europe. One Father Francois Richard produced a book concerning the island of Santorini in 1657 that describes the vrykolakas and Joseph Pitton de Tournefort recounts having seen a community destroy a body that they believed was such a being on Mykonos in 1701, published in 1718.

Striges

In ancient Roman folklore reference is made to a vampire-like being called a strix, the plural of the word being 'striges'. The concept derives from a legendary ancient Greek creature whose name means 'screecher' and was commonly associated with owls. In a story that is very similar to that of Lycaon who was transformed into a wolf for having eaten human flesh a woman called Polyphonte was turned into a strix in an ancient Greek story. The strix is usually described as a person who is able in some way to change their form, and preys upon humans and drinks their blood. The association with the obviously deep fear of the night habits of owls appears to be widespread in ancient beliefs. It is interesting to note that the taxonomist Carl Linnaeus established the genus strix to describe and classify earless owls in 1758, drawing on this expression. It was also used, albeit incorrectly, as a common scientific term for other types of owls.

The Eucharist

There are a number of passages within the Bible that place a taboo on the act of consuming blood with the implication that to do otherwise is in direct contravention of God's laws. In *Deuteronomy* 12:23, for example, it says, 'Only be sure that you do not eat the blood; for the blood is the life, and you shall not eat the life with the meat'.

A comparable passage from *Leviticus* states that, 'For the life of the flesh is in the blood…therefore I said unto the children of Israel, "No soul of you shall eat blood, neither shall any stranger that sojourneth among you eat blood."' *Leviticus* 17:11-12.

In a key passage from *Dracula* an almost identical comment is made by Renfield the zoophagous patient at the lunatic asylum run by Dr Seward when he laps up blood that has fallen from the injured wrist of the doctor, 'The blood is the life! The blood is the life!' (Bram Stoker, *Dracula*, Oxford University Press, 1998 edition, p141).

Blood is of course symbolic of physical vitality and life but to see it flowing from a wound is an indication of danger and a loss of the life force. In the Greek cult of the god Dionysus red wine was drunk by his followers as symbolic of consuming his blood. Dionysus was credited with giving the vine to humanity. Within the Christian tradition the ritual of the Eucharist where Christians drink wine and eat the wafer is symbolic of the blood and flesh of Christ. It is both an act of commemoration and spiritual renewal and unification with God.

The Vampire and Medieval European Folklore

During the middle ages there was a widespread belief in the existence of incubi and succubi. An incubus was a male demon that was supposed to lie on top of sleeping women and have sex with them. It is thought that this was often given as an excuse for unwanted pregnancies but nonetheless many in the Catholic and Orthodox Churches believed in their existence. The female equivalent of the incubus was the succubus, which was also thought to be a demon that took human shape in order to have sex with men. In the treatise on witches called *Malleus Maleficarum* or *Hammer of the Witches*, written in 1486 by Heinrich Kramer and Jacob Sprenger, it was claimed that the succubi gathered semen from men which they then passed on to the incubi who would impregnate women with it. It was often believed that children who were born with deformations or abnormalities were a result of these demons and that they were also open to the influence of evil spirits. Such ideas would also influence the belief in vampires and both ideas share a common concern with night-time predation on sleeping victims and the draining of their energies.

Revenants

The concept of the vampire has much in common with the medieval belief in the revenant. A 'revenant' was the name given to a corpse or spirit that was believed to have returned from the grave to trouble living people. The idea of the revenant arose particularly in Western Europe, although it has clear parallels with similar concepts from other cultures. There are a number of distinguishing themes in tales of revenants.

They generally feature an individual who is identified as having been impious or done some form of wrong, someone who has committed bad deeds in life and who returns from the grave to attack members of their community or bring sickness to the living.

A number of examples have survived of medieval chroniclers, such as William of Newburgh whose work dates from around the twelfth century, who describe instances of revenants returning to haunt the living. Although vampires have in folkloric belief often been thought to have been people who in life were heretics or witches there are other reasons given for their transformation after death. In the folklore of many Slavic countries it was said that, if a dog or a cat was to jump over the body of a corpse, then this could create a vampire. An interesting method for controlling vampires was to scatter grain, sand or seeds around their graves because when they arose to feed on the living they would be compelled to stop and count them all.

There are a number of charms or items which are said to deter revenants. Although there is variation in these they are often said to include holy water and garlic. Garlic was arranged around important entrances such as windows, chimneys and doors. Famously vampires were said to be repelled by crucifixes and rosaries. The appropriate way to destroy a vampire was by driving a wooden stake through its heart. There are some interesting parallels between the act of staking a vampire and the symbolism of the Christian warrior martyr St George who famously slew the dragon, a potent symbol of evil, by driving a lance into its mouth before beheading it. As we shall see, the eve of St George's Day, 23 April, was believed in Eastern Europe to be the time when vampires and evil creatures held full sway.

Bram Stoker included this folkloric reference in *Dracula* and it is also interesting to note that Vlad

Dracula, the Wallachian medieval nobleman from whom Stoker took the name for his character (see Chapter Six), was a member of a chivalric order of the Dragon of St George.

Feast of St George

In Chapter One of *Dracula* the young English solicitor Jonathan Harker, who is travelling to Transylvania to assist the count in acquiring properties in England, is warned that he should not travel on the eve of St George's Day. He is staying in the Golden Krone hotel in Bistritz before travelling on to Dracula's Castle and, when he questions the hotel landlord and his wife about the count, they are strangely reticent, pretending not to understand his German and crossing themselves. However, just as he is about to set out on his fateful journey the landlord's wife begs him to stay.

When he asks why she answers, 'It is the eve of St George's Day. Do you know that tonight, when the clock strikes midnight, all the evil things in the world will have full sway? Do you know where you are going, and what you are going to?' (Bram Stoker, *Dracula*, Oxford University Press, 1998 edition, p5). Failing to persuade Harker to delay his journey for a couple of days the landlady insists that he take a crucifix and wear it, 'For your mother's sake', although as an English Protestant he feels uncomfortable with this Catholic rosary.

St George is perhaps best known today as the patron saint of England whose popularity reached its apogee during the medieval period. There is considerable debate as to whether a real St George existed at all, although in the earliest hagiographies relating his life he is commonly referred to as a Roman citizen of high standing, perhaps serving in the Roman army, who was martyred as a Christian for refusing to deny his faith on 23 April 303 AD. His principal shrine is located at a town in Israel that is today known as Lod but which was formerly Lydda, believed by many to be the site of his death. During the Middle Ages a legend developed around this early Christian martyr: that he was a knight who famously slew a dragon that was terrorising the city of Silene in Libya. This legend was crystallised in *The Golden Legend*, a compilation of the lives of the Christian saints compiled by Jacobus de Voragine, Archbishop of Genoa, in 1275. It was published as an English edition in 1485.

In Stoker's narrative Jonathan Harker is using the English Gregorian calendar and therefore establishes the date as 4 May. However, the inhabitants of

Transylvania at the time of the novel's writing are using the Julian calendar and in this region it is therefore 22 April. The importance of this date is that in Eastern European folklore it is believed that vampires are at their most active and terrible on the eve of St George's Day and also the eve of the feast day of St Andrew.

Walpurgis Night

Another significant religious festival that features a combination of pagan and Christian elements is that of Walpurgis Night. In Bram Stoker's short story 'Dracula's Guest' (see Chapter Six), now thought to have been the original 'missing' first chapter of *Dracula*, a young Englishman finds himself alone beside a tomb in the deserted countryside close to Munich on Walpurgis Night. With a shock the young man remembers that on Walpurgis Night, 'according to the belief of millions of people, the devil was abroad – when the graves were opened and the dead came forth and walked. When all evil things of the earth and air and water held revel' (Bram Stoker, 'Dracula's Guest', p11). At the beginning of the 1931 film version of *Dracula*, memorably starring Bela Lugosi, a Romanian peasant observes that it is Walpurgis Night.

The festival of Walpurgis Night takes place on the night of 30 April through to 1 May. It takes its name from the feast of St Walburga, also referred to in Europe as Walpurgis or Vauborg, who was born in Devon around 710 AD. She achieved lasting fame as an Anglo-Saxon nun who travelled to Germany and assisted St Boniface in his missionary work there. She became the Abbess of the monastery of Heidenheim that had been established by her brother Willibald. Although St Walburga died on 25 February 779 AD, and this is her main feast day as recorded in the Roman Martyrology, her relics were later translated to Eichstätt on 1 May 870 AD. Her other brother Winnibald had been buried there in 776 AD and she was placed alongside him.

However, 1 May had previously long been an important date in pre-Christian pagan cultures as a celebration of spring. It was believed to be a time in the ritual year when the division between the worlds of the living and the dead was particularly weak, and traditionally bonfires were lit on Walpurgis Night to keep away the evil spirits. In Norse culture the god Odin was believed to have hung himself upon the world tree of Yggdrasil in order to gain knowledge and to have briefly died on this night but been reborn with the coming of May Day.

It was believed in Germany that on the night of 30 April witches would meet together on the Brocken Mountain and hold unholy revels there. This is the highest peak of the Harz Mountains in north central Germany and is associated with a curious natural phenomenon called the Brocken spectre. When the sun is low if a person stands upon the Brocken Mountain their shadow becomes unusually magnified and projected onto clouds and is often surrounded by strange rainbow-coloured bands.

Chapter Two

The Vampire in World Folklore

As we have seen a belief in vampiric creatures that drink the blood of the living appears to be an ancient one. An interesting early example of this consists of surviving ancient Persian shards of pottery that appear to show some form of mysterious demons that attack men to drink their blood. In Chinese folklore it was believed that an individual could become a vampire if a dog or cat jumped over their corpse in a clear parallel with some European beliefs. It was also thought that, if a vampire encountered a sack of rice, its nature would force it to count each grain of rice.

There are a number of vampire-like creatures in the myths and legends of Africa. For example, a number of tribes in South Africa spoke of the Impundulu, a word that translates as 'lightning bird'. This terrifying bird was said to be black and white in appearance and able to produce thunder and lightning. It was claimed that the Impundulu was under the control of a witch doctor or witch and was used by them to attack their enemies. In another interesting parallel to European beliefs about vampiric creatures it was said to sometimes transform itself into an attractive young man so that it could drink the blood of young women. In West Africa the Ashanti have stories of the frightening figure of the Asanbosam. This vampiric creature is said to possess iron teeth and was in the habit of living in trees from which it would launch itself at potential victims.

Egyptian Vampires

It is interesting to note that the ancient mythology of Egypt also features a deity that can be seen today as strongly vampiric in character. The fierce goddess of Upper Egypt, Sekhmet, has a number of legends associated with her cult that are reminiscent of the modern concept of the vampire. (There are a number of variations in the spelling of her name including Sakhmat and Sekhet.) She is a figure associated with the sun and was seen as a powerful warrior and was famed for her prowess as a hunter. In keeping with Sekhmet's identification with the theme of hunting she was often portrayed in the form of a lioness.

According to Egyptian mythology Sekhmet was

so powerful that her breath alone was responsible for forming the desert. Interestingly, it was believed that Sekhmet had helped the people of Upper Egypt conquer the inhabitants of Lower Egypt and had defeated their goddess who was called Bast. The name Sekhmet translates as 'the one who is powerful'. Because she had helped conquer Lower Egypt she was referred to as the 'scarlet lady'. This signified the blood that had been spilt in battle and her blood rage when fighting. However, it was also linked to female menstruation as she was viewed by women as the goddess of this aspect of female life.

The pharaohs of Egypt believed that Sekhmet would aid them in times of war and act as their particular guardian against injuries sustained during fighting. It was believed that Sekhmet could be called upon to help cure different illnesses and her name became a term used by Egyptians to refer to people who worked as medical practitioners. On a darker more sinister level it was also believed that, if angered, Sekhmet could unleash terrible afflictions and woes upon the population. For this reason the priestesses who served the goddess carried out daily rituals to maintain her good favour.

In a legend particularly resonant in a study of vampirism Sekhmet was believed to save the ancient

Egyptians during the annual flooding of the mighty river Nile.

It is thought that during this yearly event the colour of the Nile would alter to a vivid red colour, reminiscent of the colour of blood, because of silt being washed into the river. The ancient Egyptians thought that Sekhmet drank the red waters each year and so saved her followers from destruction.

This potent myth is thought to have inspired or influenced an important annual festival which the Egyptians held in her honour. During the festival participants would hold lively celebrations involving dancing and most importantly drinking.

By drinking an excess of beer the followers of Sekhmet were attempting to pacify the anger of the warrior goddess, and celebrating and recognising her role in drinking the blood-red floodwater of the life-giving but potentially destructive Nile.

Interestingly, excavations at a temple linked to the cult of Sekhmet who was later merged with other similar mythological figures identified a so-called 'porch of drunkenness', constructed during the reign of the female pharaoh called Hatshepsut (1508 BC-1458 BC).

Penanggalan

A particularly grotesque and macabre variation on the theme of vampirism is the folkloric creature called the Penanggalan. Originating in the Malay Peninsula this unusual form of vampire is said to be a female head that has been separated from its body and is able to fly. When the Penanggalan is in flight it is claimed that its entrails hang beneath it. There are also strong parallels between this vampiric figure and the Manananggal which is found in the folklore of the Philippines. However, the Penanggalan is distinct in that, when the head is detached from the body, it takes with it the stomach, intestines and the lungs. It is generally believed that a Penanggalan is a midwife who makes a deal with the devil in order to gain magical power.

It is a common feature of these folkloric stories that the woman in question breaks the deal, often by eating meat, which she has promised the devil that she will not do for a period of 40 days. As punishment the devil forces her to become a vampire that detaches its head and entrails from its body. It is said that the midwife must soak her entrails in a container of vinegar in order to shrink them sufficiently to put them back inside her body. Typically, the victims of the Penanggalan are children and pregnant women whose blood she feeds on. It is claimed that she appears when a woman is giving birth and will attempt to drink the mother's blood with her tongue which is magically invisible.

A traditional way of keeping the Penanggalans at bay is by placing thorns around the houses of pregnant women in order that the monster will become caught on them and then killed. Interestingly, it is said that when the Penanggalans are flying at night their dangling entrails resemble the lights of fireflies.

A similar and probably connected figure with the qualities of a vampire is the Leyak of Balinese culture. The Leyak also takes the form of a flying head whose entrails hang beneath it. Like the Penanggalan it flies through the air looking for pregnant women in order to drink the blood of their babies. It is said that Leyak are human beings who have become monsters by practising black magic. It is also said that they are cannibals and frequent graveyards, feeding on the bodies of the dead. In appearance the Leyak head has a particularly long tongue and the long fangs associated with European vampires. Leyaks are believed to be the followers of a death goddess figure called Rangda. She is termed the Queen of the Leyak and is described as being a widow-witch. During certain festivals a mask that depicts her features is displayed and Leyak statues can be found in domestic settings in Bali.

Indian Vampires

The ancient Hindu goddess Kali has particularly strong associations with death and is often portrayed as bloodthirsty and destructive. She is often represented wielding a sword and wearing human skulls as a grotesque decoration and has a frightening appearance, complete with red eyes and lolling tongue. Interestingly, although Kali is linked particularly closely with the themes of death and destruction, she is more properly viewed as a goddess who symbolises the inevitable cycles of life and change. Kali can be said to represent, on a more profound level, time and mortality, and her terrifying figure is intended to provoke an awareness of these harsh but unavoidable realities in humanity.

In the religious text called the Markandeya Purana, Kali is described as having appeared from the forehead of another goddess called Durga in a battle between the forces of the anti-divine and divine powers.

The best-known story from Hindu culture concerning Kali has strongly vampiric overtones to modern readers. The story begins with a battle between the goddess Durga and a ferocious demon called Raktabija. Durga is aided in this attack by the Matrikas but although they manage to inflict many wounds on the body of Raktabija they cannot defeat him. This is because each drop of blood that the demon sheds is miraculously transformed into another replica of Raktabija and Durga and her helpers find themselves facing an enemy growing in strength.

According to one tradition Durga calls upon Kali for help in this supernatural contest and Kali springs from her forehead carrying a sword in one hand and a noose in the other. She is said to be terrifying to look upon with wild crazed hair, red eyes and gaping mouth. Clad in a tiger skin, Kali leaps roaring into battle and destroys Raktabija by sucking his body dry of blood and then feasting upon his offspring.

Following her victory Kali is said to dance upon the bodies of the dead on the battlefield. She is said to have become drunk on the blood of her victims to the extent that she is unaware that her own husband Shiva is lying amongst the bodies of fallen warriors. However, Shiva calls out to Kali and when she hears him her fury is diminished and she is ashamed.

Hindu mythology also talks of the churel which is a kind of vampiric ghost. It is said that it is created after a woman has died whilst giving birth or through menstruation. As revenge for this the churel is thought to specifically attack young men and drink their blood. The churel apparently takes two distinct and opposing forms. It is said sometimes to appear as a youthful woman of great beauty in order to entrap men. However, it is also said to appear as an unkempt and horrible figure with a strange, long black tongue. Commonly, the churel is thought to be found close to streams or rivers. An alternative belief concerning the churel is that it is the spirit of a woman who has gained power through some form of dark magic and, as in the European vampire myth, its body is often said to be absent from its place of burial.

Lycanthropy

Wolves play a particularly significant role in Bram Stoker's *Dracula*. Perhaps most famously, whilst Count Dracula is entertaining the young English estate agent Jonathan Harker at his castle in Transylvania, he pauses to listen to them howling outside. In an aside to Harker he comments:

'Listen to them – the children of the night. What music they make!' (Bram Stoker, *Dracula*, Oxford University Press, 1998 edition, p18).

Dracula is also able to exert control over wolves and they follow and encircle Jonathan Harker on his coach journey to Castle Dracula. They also figure prominently in the closing pursuit of Dracula by Van Helsing and Jonathan Harker's friends and companions. In the short story 'Dracula's Guest' by Bram Stoker (see Chapter Six) there is some inference that a large wolf that appears within the story is actually the vampiric count transformed. When the Russian schooner the *Demeter* out of Varna is driven onto the sand banks of Whitby in *Dracula*, astonished local witnesses report seeing a large black dog leap off the ship and onto the shoreline before racing off into the darkness. The strange black dog is, of course, Dracula himself, who we learn is able to shape-shift into animals such as a dog and, more famously, a bat. Dracula can also transform his shape into a mist or even particles that can drift magically through windows. Later in the novel a wolf from London zoo known as Berserker is reported to have escaped from its enclosure under the supernatural influence of the count.

Werewolves or lycanthropes can be found in a number of world mythologies from different cultures. Today in popular culture a werewolf is a mythical figure that is generally perceived to be a human being who is able to change shape into the form of a wolf. Generally in folklore and horror fiction the werewolf is believed to have inherited some form of family curse or to have become a werewolf because they have been bitten by another werewolf who has passed on the condition to them. There are parallels here between this and the bite of a vampire creating new vampires in a kind of supernatural epidemic like the spreading of a virus.

One of the earliest references to the concept of men altering their shape and taking on that of a wolf in a transformation triggered by a full moon can be found in the ancient Greek world. Herodotus describes men changing into wolves in his Histories and Pausanias tells the story of King Lycaon of Arcadia who was punished by Zeus by being turned into a wolf for sacrificing a child on his altar.

Another striking example of the werewolf as described in ancient sources can be found in the writings of the Roman poet Ovid. He describes the mythological character of Lycaon as shape-shifting into a wolf and attacking flocks of sheep.

However, the first reliable written example of the use of the term werewolf appears in 1212. It can be found in *Otia Imperialia*, a medieval text written by Gervase of Tilbury. It is thought that the origin of the term werewolf derives from Old English. Clearly the second part of the phrase indicates wolf and is derived from the earlier term 'wulf' whilst 'wer' or sometimes 'were' is an Old English word meaning 'man'.

Quite how the belief in werewolves began is a question that has been the subject of a great deal of speculation. From a rational, logical perspective it could be said that werewolves, like vampires, are monsters created by people at times as a kind of coping mechanism to explain truly horrific but undeniably human behaviour such as the atrocities of serial killers. The author Sabine Baring-Gould amongst others has explored this argument. But it is also interesting and useful to examine the role of the wolf in European and world folklore and its relationship to man. Until relatively recent times the wolf was greatly feared by people because it represented a potentially lethal predator that from time to time preyed upon human populations. It comes as little surprise then to find this animal combined with the most frightening stories told in popular legends and mythology.

It has also been observed that other cultures have equivalents of the European concept of the werewolf such as the Indian weretiger and the werejaguar of South America.

In these contexts the animal whose identity has been merged into local folklore is one that is (potentially) particularly dangerous to human beings. Interestingly, in Viking culture warriors who wore animal hides during battle were believed to be able to invoke their ferocious nature making them fearsome adversaries. Perhaps the most famous examples of this are the berserkers who wore the skins of bears when fighting. However, the Ulfhednar were warriors who dressed in wolf skins and were reputed to be terrible opponents who did not appear to feel pain and fought like wild animals.

The French term used to describe a werewolf is 'loup-garou' and there are many examples of a belief in werewolf attacks in French history. 'Loup' is the French word for 'wolf' and derives from the Latin 'Lupus' and 'garoul' is an Old French word that, in fact, meant 'werewolf'. One of the most striking and famous examples of wolf attacks fuelling a belief in werewolves occurred in south central France between the years 1764 and 1767. The predations against humans by the so-called Beast of Gevaudan were particularly savage and it is thought that more than 80 people were killed by one or more wolves during this awful period. The first attack took place during the summer of 1764 in the area known then as Gévaudan and which today is called Lozère. A woman who was tending a herd of cattle in this mountainous region was suddenly attacked by a very large wolf. However, her life was saved because some of the cattle that she was watching over appear to have driven off the predator, instinctively protecting the herd. The woman was still badly injured by the attack and only a few weeks later a wolf attacked another person. This time the attack was to prove fatal as a 14-year-old girl was killed by the animal close to the small village of Hubacs.

The wolf was to strike again on 12 January 1765 when it attacked a group of children that included Jacques Portefaix and six friends, two of whom were girls. However, three of the older children struck at the wolf with sticks and stones and, by staying together, managed to drive it away even though some of the children were bitten during the attack. The story of their bravery was brought to the attention of King Louis XV who gave rewards of money to the children and also granted that Portefaix be given an education paid for by the state. Most importantly he instructed that a professional wolf hunter be sent to kill the Beast of Gevaudan. Jean-Charles Marc-Antoine Vaumesle d'Enneval was chosen for the job and he travelled to the region with his son Jean-Francois. Although they hunted wolves in the area the attacks continued to take place and the task was passed onto François Antoine in June 1765.

He appeared to have more success, killing a particularly large wolf on 21 September that was believed to be the culprit behind the attacks. Although he was rewarded for his actions, another attack took place on 2 December 1765 in which two children were injured. The attacks continued until 1767 when a local hunter called Jean Chastel finally killed the animal, a larger than normal wolf with reddish fur. Fictionalised accounts of the kill claimed that Chastel had used a silver bullet to dispatch his quarry. Others claimed that Chastel had in fact trained the beast and was behind the killings. In recent years two different films have been inspired by the Beast of Gevaudan: *Brotherhood of the Wolf* (2001) and *La Bête du Gévaudan* (2003).

A number of modern writers including Richard H. Thompson have argued that the attacks can be explained as matching known wolf behaviour. Some have claimed that wolves of this period were more aggressive than modern wolves because natural selection has meant that wolves have 'learned' to avoid people because of the risk of being killed with guns. It has also been observed that when wolf attacks take place in the modern era it is generally in areas suffering from poverty where populations are not able to defend themselves. Another theory is that the large stature of the wolves and their strange reddish colouring is due to them having been a cross-breed of dog and wolf. Hybrid breeds of wolf-dogs have been observed in the former Soviet Union and they are often larger than wolves and do not have a natural fear of human beings.

Werewolf Transformation

Today most people associate lycanthropy with an individual victim having been bitten by another werewolf who passes on their condition like a kind of virus. However, in many cases of folklore and legend in the past this was not the case. An interesting example of how individuals became a werewolf can be found in Portuguese and Brazilian culture. It used to be believed that the seventh son in a family would become a werewolf whilst the seventh daughter was doomed to be a witch. In Northern Argentina this belief was so strong that in 1920 a law was passed aimed at changing perceptions regarding the unlucky nature of the seventh son. It was common for these unfortunate children to actually be abandoned or even murdered and so the government introduced a law stating that the President of Argentina should be recognised as the godfather of these seventh sons born to families. The seventh son would then be provided with a gold medal at their baptism and crucially would then be provided with a scholarship up until the age of 21. The law largely helped change attitudes about seventh sons.

Other accounts particularly from the medieval period ascribe lycanthropy to satanic practices. There are also stories from folklore in which different saints punish individuals by transforming them into wolves. One of the most famous examples involves St Patrick, the patron saint of Ireland, who was said to have turned the body of King Vereticus into that of a wolf. It is also commonly believed that the full moon triggers the transformation of werewolves and that the individual in question is powerless to stop it. According to folklore the plant wolfsbane can help deter werewolves. Mistletoe and rye are also said to be effective against them. And it has become a staple of novels and films that werewolves can be killed with a silver bullet or knife.

In more recent years there have been some attempts to explain a belief in werewolves by scientists who argue that certain medical conditions could have been wrongly interpreted in the past as lycanthropy. For example people who suffered from epilepsy were sometimes branded as werewolves in superstitious societies.

In 1963 Dr Lee Illis of Guy's Hospital in London produced a paper entitled *On Porphyria and the Aetiology of Werewolves.* In this paper Dr Illis argued that people in more primitive and superstitious times had labelled sufferers of the condition of congenital porphyria as werewolves. The symptoms of this condition include reddish teeth, an aversion to light and mental health problems. It has also been suggested that legends and myths concerning werewolves could actually be linked to the real virus of rabies that is transmitted through the bite of a person or animal with the disease.

Werewolves have, perhaps unsurprisingly, been often linked to vampires in folklore as well as horror fiction. In Greece, as late as the end of the nineteenth century, some superstitions claimed that if the bodies of werewolves were not destroyed they would become undead vampires. As we have seen, within many Slavic languages, vampires and werewolves were given the name Vulkodlak, the same collective term for both forms of monster.

South American Vampires

Throughout the Caribbean islands and in parts of the southern United States there are tales of a monster known as the Loogaroo. The Loogaroo is thought to be a witch who serves the devil. The witch takes blood from her victims in order to keep the favour of the devil. If she fails to find the blood of others, she is compelled to give her own, resulting in her death. Sometimes taking the form of a ball of blue fire, the Loogaroo haunts the night, searching for victims to drain of their blood. According to folklore she leaves her skin beneath a silk cotton tree and collects it after transforming from the ball of blue light.

It is claimed that the Loogaroo like other similar vampiric monsters has a compulsion to count grains of seed or sand and so it was thought that leaving a pile of grains in front of your front door would stop her crossing the threshold. It is thought that the word 'Loogaroo' may be a corruption of 'loup-garou', the French term for a werewolf. It appears that the folk beliefs of France and the voodoo beliefs of the slave populations taken from Africa have combined to produce this mythical being.

Vampire Bats

Although bats have become synonymous with the vampire legend for modern audiences, it was only after the discovery of the Americas during the sixteenth century that they were incorporated into vampire folklore. In Chapter Twelve of *Dracula*, the American adventurer Quincey Morris makes a connection between the effects of loss of blood from Lucy Westenra and his experiences in South America. After seeing how exhausted and shattered Arthur Holmwood has become after giving blood via a transfusion to save Lucy, he observes that, 'I have not seen anything pulled down so quick since I was on the Pampas and had a mare that I was fond of go to grass all in a night. One of those big bats that they call vampires had got at her in the night, and what with his gorge and the vein left open there wasn't enough blood in her to let her stand up...'(Bram Stoker, *Dracula*, Oxford University Press, 1998 edition, p151).

In Chapter Fourteen (p.205), Stoker also has Professor Van Helsing refer to bats in the Pampas preying on cattle and horses and how, in the islands of the Western Seas, there are bats that prey on sailors, draining them of their blood. However, vampire bats are not found in the Western Seas. Also the graphic description of the habits of the vampire bat made by Quincey Morris is something of a melodramatic exaggeration of the reality.

There are in fact three species of vampire bat found in the Americas that feed on blood. They are the common vampire bat, the hairy-legged vampire bat and the white-winged vampire bat. The common vampire bat will feed on most warm-blooded animals whilst the white-winged vampire bat has apparently a taste for goats and birds. Typically a vampire bat will locate a potential host while it is sleeping and approach it from the ground using its strong and unusually long legs to leap onto a vulnerable part of its victim rather than landing from flight. Vampire bats do not, as mythology would suggest, suck the blood from their victims but use their sharp teeth to bite them and create a wound from which the blood flows. They then lick and lap up the blood as it leaves the wound. Importantly their saliva contains anticoagulants that keep the blood flowing and also appear to have anaesthetic properties.

Before the arrival of Europeans to the Americas the vampire bat was in fact revered in Central America as a bat god called Camazotz who dwelt in caves and in mythology lived in the bathhouse of the Underworld. It is thought that Europeans made the connection between the habits of the vampire bat and the vampire of European folklore, naming it after their own mythical monsters.

In Bram Stoker's *Dracula* the count is able to shape-shift into the forms of a dog or wolf and also into a strange mist or column of particles. It was not until the 1927 stage production of the novel that bats were introduced into the Dracula mythology. In the 1931 film adaptation of *Dracula* starring Bela Lugosi as the count he is shown transforming into a bat and it has become a common image since then. Because vampire bats are rather small the flying fox bat has often been used as a stand-in by filmmakers because of its greater size. Although bats have been linked to the supernatural in Europe because of their night-time habits the concept of vampiric activity was more commonly linked to the imagined night behaviour of owls. There are no species of vampire bat in Europe.

Chupacabra

One of the most striking examples of a belief in vampirism to emerge in recent years involves wide-ranging reports of a mysterious creature known as the Chupacabra. It has been claimed that some kind of unknown animal has been attacking livestock in Central and North America. The creature in question is said to be particularly fond of attacking goats and feasting on their blood. Indeed the name chupacabra is derived from the Spanish term 'chupar' that means 'to suck' and the word 'cabra', meaning goat. Combined together the literal translation of the name of this elusive animal is 'goatsucker'! The term is said to have been invented by a comedian from Puerto Rico called Silverio Perez following the first reports of vampiric type attacks on animals in Central America.

Perhaps the earliest account of the chupacabra dates from March 1995 when eight sheep were found dead of mysterious causes in Puerto Rico. Each animal appeared to have suffered from three puncture wounds to the chest and their corpses were completely bloodless. Later that same year the chupacabra was reported to have struck again at Canóvanas, a municipality in the same country. It was claimed that it had drained the blood of up to 150 local animals including not only farm livestock but also people's pets.

Further reports began to emerge in the aftermath of these killings across a wide geographical area including Argentina, Brazil, Honduras, Mexico and the USA as well as many other Central American regions. Commonly, alleged sightings of the creature appear to combine a bizarre mix of physical characteristics. It is said be around three or four feet tall and has something of the appearance of a kangaroo, and stands on two feet. It is, however, also said to be reptilian-looking and many have commented that it has a row of spines that run from its neck along its back to the base of its tail. It is also characterised as possessing prominent fangs and a forked tongue. It has also been claimed that the chupacabra has unusual red and glowing eyes. However, a divergent tradition has emerged in which the chupacabra is claimed to resemble a dog with reptilian characteristics.

The hysteria surrounding the chupacabra appeared to have jumped continents when, in April 2006, it was reported that the beast had struck in Russia. It was claimed that in the previous year something had been killing animals and draining their blood.

In particular sheep and turkeys had been attacked and their blood sucked dry.

Back in the USA, in a report reminiscent of a Stephen King storyline, the partially decomposed body of a strange animal killed on a road in Maine was claimed to be the culprit responsible for attacking a number of dogs and corresponded to local sightings of a mysterious creature.

Attacks on chickens in Cuero, Texas also appeared to have the hallmarks of the chupacabra. However, a more rational explanation appeared to have been found when the carcasses of three unusual-looking animals were discovered close to the attack site in 2007. One of the animals was analysed at the Texas State University and it was identified as a coyote with an unusual appearance, being a blue-grey colour and lacking hair. It was also observed that it had large fang-like teeth, matching many of the descriptions of the chupacabra. Since then further reports have emerged from the same region of Texas of a strange animal that corresponded to the description of the hairless coyote and apparently had noticeably shorter front legs. It has been suggested that this may indicate an established group of this strain of coyote in the area.

Chapter Three

Vlad the Impaler

There has been considerable debate about the extent to which Bram Stoker based his fictional character of Count Dracula on the real life figure of Vlad Tepes. The name Vlad Tepes is Romanian for 'Vlad the Impaler' a moniker derived from his alleged favourite means of dispatching his rivals and enemies. He was a medieval Wallachian 'voivode' or nobleman who reigned over an area that is today part of southern Romania. It is interesting to note that the Ottoman Turks, with whom he was to spend much of his life in conflict, also referred to him as 'Kazikli Bey' which translates as Impaler Prince. Vlad Tepes whose formal name was Vladislav III Dracula held power in Wallachia at three different times in his life – firstly in 1448, then from 1456 to 1462, and lastly in 1476. He has come to be viewed as a ruler who meted out harsh and inhumanly cruel forms of 'justice' to his opponents and to those who disobeyed him. However, it must be remembered that Vlad lived in particularly savage and brutal times and it has been argued that his methods of ruling his country were, in fact, no worse than many other medieval rulers. In his native Romania, Vlad is viewed by many as something of a hero, a strong ruler who defended his country from foreign invasion and who demanded honesty and fairness from his people albeit by imposing vicious punishments against transgressors.

It is thought that Vladislav III was born during the winter of 1431 at the fortress of Sighişoara in Transylvania. His father was Vladislav II also known as Vlad Dracul and the identity of his mother was disputed but he was raised by Princess Cneajna of Moldavia who was married to his father. Vladislav III was the second of three sons, the eldest being Mircea and the youngest known as Radu the Handsome. The surname of Dracula was inherited by Vlad the Impaler from his father's title of Vlad Dracul. It indicates that he is the son of Vlad Dracul. In the Romanian language today 'dracul' means 'devil' but in old Romanian it also meant 'dragon'. Vlad the Impaler's father was a member of the chivalric crusading order that swore to protect Christendom from the Muslim Ottoman Turks called the Order of the Dragon (of St George).

Vlad II Dracul is thought to have been born in around 1395 and he was the illegitimate son of a ruler of Wallachia called Mircea the Elder. It is important to note that in Wallachia the line of succession for the throne of the country did not simply move from father to son. Instead influential nobles known as boyars would actually elect the Prince of Wallachia. It was required that candidates be from voivode families but this also included those born illegitimately. This system of rule would greatly influence the reign of Vlad Tepes because it meant that in the past the boyars had tremendous power in Wallachia and that many rulers had been deposed and murdered by warring factions. The two major factions in the time of Vlad II were the descendants of Mircea the Elder of which he was one and the descendants of a prince called Dan II who took the name of the Danesti. Geographically and politically Wallachia was also positioned between the two major powers of the Kingdom of Hungary and the ever expanding and seemingly unstoppable Ottoman Empire.

Vlad II had been part of the court of the Holy Roman Emperor, Sigismund, King of Hungary. It was with the backing of Sigismund that Vlad II became prince of Wallachia in 1436. As mentioned earlier in this chapter he had been inducted into the Order of the Dragon in 1431. Sigismund also enlisted other Eastern European rulers to the order from Serbia and Poland and its aim was to protect the Holy Roman Empire and the vulnerable territories of Eastern Europe from the incursions of the Ottoman Empire.

The Order of the Dragon

In 1408 King Sigismund had refounded the chivalric elite of the Order of the Dragon. The 24 noblemen who joined the order by the invitation of Sigismund would defend and support the king and his heirs whilst also agreeing to fight in defence of the Catholic faith. The enemies of the Order were seen to be heretics, pagans and those plotting against the king in order to gain his territory. The greatest threat to the power of Sigismund was from the encroachments of the Turks and the re-foundation of the Order of the Dragon can be seen largely as a response to their territorial expansion.

The insignia of the order was the image of a dragon with its tail coiled around its neck. On the back of the dragon appeared the motif of the cross. Radu R Florescu describes the cross as 'similar to the cross of Lorraine adopted by Joan of Arc' (Radu R Florescu, *Dracula: Prince of Many Faces*, p40). Others have viewed the motif as similar to the iconography of the story of St George and the dragon with the appearance of the cross on the back of the dragon representing the triumph of Christianity over its enemies.

Members of the order were known as Draconists and, according to Florescu, were distinguished by the adoption of related garments and insignia. These are said to have included two different capes of differing colours. One was green in colour and supposed to represent the scaly skin of the dragon whilst underneath some form of red garment was worn that represented the blood of the Christian martyrs. On Fridays or during the commemoration of the passion of Christ, members of the Order of the Dragon were required to wear a black cape that Florescu argues was the inspiration for the famous cloak worn by Stoker's Count Dracula. Vlad II was to incorporate the image of the dragon into his own personal insignia.

However, Vlad II found himself in the often difficult position of having to mediate and make deals with both the Hungarian superpower and, at other times, the Ottomans. In about 1443, Vlad II handed over his sons Vlad III, the future Vlad the Impaler, and his younger brother, Radu the Handsome, to the court of the Sultan Murad II as hostages to guarantee that he would not take up arms against the Ottomans. He took an oath to this effect that he swore on a copy of the Koran. Vlad and his brother were held hostage until 1448. They would have had comparative freedom of movement but always under the shadow of the possibility of execution. It was a fairly common practice of this period for nobles to give their relatives as a sign of faith. Many have argued that it was this confinement that was to result in Vlad Tepes's hatred for the Ottomans and his capacity for cruelty.

Some claim that his taste for impalement as a means of punishment was learned from the Turks and on later occasions inflicted on them.

Vlad II was removed from power by John Hunyadi, the elected regent of Hungary at this time, who had him killed in December 1447. Hunyadi attacked the capital of Tirgovişte (today known as Targovişte) where Vlad II and his elder son Mircea were present, intent on replacing them with a member of the Danesti. When the capital was besieged by Hunyadi's forces, the Boyars in the city betrayed their rulers and captured Mircea, the eldest brother of Vlad Tepes, and tortured him before blinding him with red hot iron stakes and burying him alive. This horrifying episode has of course parallels with Bram Stoker's fictional creation where vampires rise from their coffins to prey on the living and are killed with stakes through their hearts.

As will be discussed in later chapters, Stoker's

Dracula is (despite the fame of this myth) killed not by a wooden stake but by a knife plunged through his heart and by being simultaneously beheaded. It is said that Vlad II Dracul was captured by members of the Danesti faction who beheaded him. However, following the murder of Vlad II and Mircea, the Ottomans invaded Wallachia in order to maintain their own power in that region. Vlad III was put on the throne of Wallachia by Murad to serve as his vassal but he was quickly removed by John Hunyadi. Vlad then sought the protection of his uncle Bogdan II of Moldavia where he stayed in exile from December 1449 to October 1451. In October 1451, Bogdan was murdered by his own brother Petru Aaron, forcing Vlad to flee Moldavia. Interestingly, Vlad would take the route of the Borgo Pass, so well known to fans of Stoker's novel, back into Wallachia where he found some shelter for a short period of time. It seems that Vlad Tepes and John Hunyadi were reconciled in 1452 and Hunyadi selected him to be the Hungarian choice for the throne of Wallachia. Plans were also drawn up for an invasion of Serbia which was at this point held by the Ottomans. The Hungarians attacked in 1456 and at the same time Vlad led an army into Wallachia. Both military actions reached their objectives and Vlad was once again Prince of Wallachia.

Vlad Tepes was to rule Wallachia again from 1456 to 1462 and his reign was to be marked by a conspicuous desire to consolidate his power. The majority of his time was spent in the city of Tirgovişte where he would often participate in criminal trials and hold court. He appears to have taken action to attempt to eliminate the threat that the boyar class held for the princes of Wallachia. It seems likely that many were murdered by Vlad for their treachery to his family in the past and he is said to have had one of those responsible for burying his brother alive taken prisoner. Legends claim that Vlad had thousands of people impaled who came from the city and who had offered refuge to his rival. He is also said to have made a rival prince give a funeral oration for himself as he knelt next to an open grave. Upon completion of the speech he was executed and buried. Vlad also undermined the old powers of the boyar class by removing them from the Prince's Council. He instead gave these financially valuable positions to individuals loyal to him and handed out knighthoods to peasant supporters, thereby surrounding himself with those who were unlikely to attack him. Vlad also (famously or infamously depending upon who is relating the tale) attacked cities and towns in the region of Transylvania that were dominated by Saxon or German or Hungarian merchants and where the local people had no power at all. The best-known Saxon pamphlets of the period describing the reign of Vlad the Impaler state that, 'In the year of our Lord 1456 Dracula did many dreadful and dangerous things', (M J Trow, *Vlad the Impaler*, p.170).

Vlad carried out raids against Braşov, known by the Germans as Kronstadt, and other towns, and had their trade privileges with Wallachia removed. This was probably motivated by a desire to further undermine the power of the old boyar class who had strong connections with them, although later commentators have chosen to view them as the actions of a patriotic ruler attempting to protect the interests of his own people from the greed of foreign merchants. Most notoriously of all, in April 1459 Vlad attacked Braşov and is said to have had 30,000 Saxons and officials impaled.

One pamphlet about the life of Vlad Dracula, printed in Nuremberg in 1499, features a woodcut that has become infamous for showing Vlad in his royal garments enjoying an open air feast at a table whilst all around him his impaled victims writhe in agony and his henchmen hack up people 'like cabbage'. The document claims that Vlad greatly enjoyed this spectacle and took great pleasure in the cruelty of his actions.

The celebration of this blood feast would continue to inform stories about his reign and it is not difficult to see how the concept of a bloodthirsty ruler could in time be linked to the concept of the vampire and their literal thirst for blood.

Between 1456 and 1459 Vlad concluded a treaty with the Sultan Mehmed the Conqueror, who had captured the city of Constantinople in 1453, that included an annual tribute. The tribute included a monetary payment to be paid annually but also involved the handing over of 500 Wallachian boys to the Ottomans who were forcibly converted to Islam from Orthodox Christianity and made to join the Janissary corps of the Ottoman army. As adults these troops were often used against Christian countries and were amongst the most fervent of the Turkish forces. From 1459 Vlad refused to pay the tribute, complaining that all his resources had been used up in controlling his kingdom but also indicating that he planned to join the Hungarian side. When an attempt was made by the Turks to take Vlad hostage, he responded by crossing into the area south of the Danube in the winter months of 1461 to 1462, razing an area that stretched from Serbia to the Black Sea. The furious Sultan raised an army that is likely to have been around 90,000 strong to attack Vlad who is thought to have commanded a force of around only 30,000.

Unable to stop such a large army entering Wallachia, Vlad instead attempted a daring attack against the camp of the Conqueror on the night of 17 June 1462, with, it seems, the intention of personally killing Mehmed in an attempt to rout the Ottoman army. Although Vlad's forces succeeded in killing several thousand Turks and came close to their objective, they ultimately failed and were forced to retreat. Mehmed may have suffered a loss of face over this attack but he nonetheless continued to advance into Wallachia. However, according to sources of the time, the morale of the Turks was given a considerable blow when the sultan's army came upon a field of stakes that held the bodies of around 20,000 victims of the wrath of Vlad Dracula.

The rotting corpses included Turkish prisoners and others of Vlad's enemies and it seems likely that the terrifying sight was intended as an act of psychological warfare on his part, with a clear message that Mehmed should turn back or suffer the same fate. However, disturbing though the sight was, the Ottoman army continued its advance and installed Vlad's brother Radu the Handsome as Prince of Wallachia, forcing the Impaler to flee the country due to lack of support.

Although he appealed to the Hungarian King Matthias Corvinus for help, it seems that Corvinus had him arrested and held prisoner, probably so that he would not be forced into outright war with the Ottomans who were now backing Vlad's brother. Legend tells that Vlad the Impaler's first wife, whose name is not known, met an unhappy end when Poenari Castle was besieged in 1462. It is said that an archer who had been a former servant to Vlad shot an arrow through one of the windows of the castle with a message attached to it, warning that the Turks were on their way, led by Radu the Handsome. The folk story relates that Vlad's wife, in desperation, threw herself from a castle tower into a tributary of the river Argeş that runs beneath the castle. She had said she would rather die and her body provide food for the fish of the river than be taken captive by the Turks. Today this body of water is referred to as the Râul Doamnei which translates as the princess's or lady's River.

Although it is known that Vlad became a prisoner of Matthias Corvinus, opinion is divided as to how long he was held captive. He was kept in relative comfort during this period which may have lasted from 1462 to 1474 in a number of different locations. He appears at one point to have been given a house in the city of Pest opposite the city of Buda across the river Danube where Corvinus held court. He enjoyed another shift in fortunes when he eventually married a cousin of Corvinus called Ilona Szilagyi. In order to do this Vlad converted from his original religion of Orthodox Christianity to Catholicism.

At this time there was a clear and definite split between the Catholic and Orthodox churches caused by the events of the Great Schism of 1054 and such a move would have been highly unpopular in his native land. It must also be remembered that Vlad is thought to have been forcibly converted to Islam during his imprisonment at the court of the Sultan. For many at the time there would have been extreme anxiety about the state of the Impaler's immortal soul and it is possible that these real historical events may have influenced subsequent legends that would surface in Stoker's novel of a prince whose soul is damned and who has turned away from God.

An anecdote from his period of confinement relates how a thief who was being chased by constables through Pest ran through the courtyard that belonged to Vlad. It is said that Vlad killed one of the constables with his sword. When later questioned as to why he had done this Vlad is said to have answered that the man committed suicide by invading the territory of a prince. In 1470, Niccolo de Modrussa who was the ambassador of Pope Pius II met Vlad the Impaler whilst he was under house arrest at the court of the king of Hungary. He carried out a number of interviews with Vlad and his documentation of his meetings with the infamous Wallachian prince provides us with a vivid first-hand snapshot of what he actually looked like.

'He was not very tall, but very stocky and strong, with a cold and terrible appearance, a strong and aquiline nose, swollen nostrils, a thin and reddish face in which the very long eyelashes framed large wide-open green eyes; the bushy black eyebrows made them appear threatening. His face and chin were shaven but for a moustache.

The swollen temples increased the bulk of his head. A bull's neck connected (with) his head from which black curly locks hung on his wide-shouldered person.' (Quoted in M J Trow, *Vlad the Impaler*, p1).

Vlad had two sons with his new wife. After the death of Radu the Handsome in 1475 another candidate for the throne of Wallachia was chosen by the Ottomans called Basarab Laiota. With the backing of the Hungarian monarch, Vlad and his cousin Prince Stephen Bathory of Moldavia invaded Wallachia with an army made up of Moldavians, rebel Transylvanians and defecting Wallachians. Vlad began his campaign on 18 July 1475 and defeated the forces of Basarab who fled to the protection of the Turks. Vlad was once again placed on the throne of Wallachia but almost immediately the bulk of the army that had supported him left with the departure of Prince Stephen who returned to Moldavia. In December 1476 Basarab Laiota, backed by the Ottoman Turks, is said by some sources to have attacked Vlad at Bucharest. There are a number of differing accounts of the death of Vlad the Impaler. Some claim that he was killed in battle close to Bucharest but it may be more likely that he was assassinated by a supporter of Basarab. According to a Russian chronicler called Kuritsyn, Vlad was surveying the battle from a hilltop when one of his own men confused him with a Turk and attacked him with a lance. In this version of events Vlad is said to have killed five men before he was killed himself. Subsequent legends also say that the head of Vlad the Impaler was cut off and sent to Constantinople where the sultan had it mounted on a stake to prove that the dreaded Dracula was dead. Tradition states that Vlad was buried at the island monastery of Snagov but, when his suspected grave was opened in 1931, it was found to be empty. It was then suggested that he had been buried not near the altar but rather near the door where people would walk on the grave. Opinion is divided as to his final resting place.

In the wake of Vlad the Impaler's reign a series of stories developed and gained popular credence through the circulation of pamphlets, often containing grotesque medieval woodcuts as illustrations. Whether there is much truth to these stories is hard to establish but they helped to create in the popular imagination his reputation for cruelty and barbarity. A close examination of them offers clues as to what kind of ruler he may have been and, just as importantly, how he was regarded by his enemies and those who sought to perpetuate propaganda against him. Significantly, it is within these same sensationalist and often horrifying documents that Vlad is often referred to simply as Dracula.

Amongst the most famous tales about the life of Vlad the Impaler is the story of the Foreign Ambassadors. There appear to be two versions of the tale, one which shows him in a fair and favourable way that is popular in Eastern Europe and another that was common in the pamphlets produced in German. In the eastern version Turkish ambassadors sent to the court of Vlad refuse to take off their turbans in his presence. When Vlad asks them why they refuse to doff their headgear in respect to him, they answer that it was not the custom of their fathers to do so. Vlad is said to have responded by ordering that the ambassadors should have their turbans nailed to their heads with three nails in order to strengthen them in their customs. For Eastern European audiences this was interpreted as showing Vlad's bravery and strength in defying the might and arrogance of the Turkish Ottoman Empire.

However, the German version, although similar, has a different emphasis. In this tale Vlad is visited at his court by ambassadors from Florence who refuse to remove their hats upon meeting him. He questions them about the matter and they reply that it is not their custom to remove their hats, claiming that they would not do so even if they were summoned before the Holy Roman Emperor. Once again Vlad is said to have had their hats nailed to their heads so that they should never be able to take them off and threw them out of his court. For audiences in Western Europe this tale was intended to show the savage and barbaric nature of the bloodthirsty prince because, in theory, diplomats were held to be immune to hostile actions and on this occasion they had been sent before him as peaceful envoys of their masters. Another popular story about the reign of Prince Vlad concerns the legend of the Golden Cup. In this tale it is claimed that, although Vlad could be a harsh and cruel ruler, his policy of impaling those who broke the law meant that Wallachia was a more honest and a safer country than it had been in the past. One day Vlad decided to test the honesty of his people by placing a cup made from gold in the main square of the city of Tirgovişte from which anyone who chose could drink water from. It is claimed that no one dared to steal the cup for fear of the wrath of Prince Vlad.

In the story of the Foreign Merchant, the emphasis is again on Vlad's insistence on honesty and the harsh justice he wielded in order to ensure lawful behaviour in his kingdom. When a foreign merchant arrives at Tirgovişte he knows that Vlad's kingdom is meant to be one where honesty and lawfulness are demanded and he leaves a wagon filled with gold ducats unattended overnight. The following morning the merchant returns to find that 160 gold ducats have disappeared. The merchant tells Vlad of the missing gold and he promises that it will be returned to him. In a severe and uncompromising statement Vlad issues the ultimatum to the people of Tirgovişte that if the money is not returned and the thief handed over he will completely destroy the city. He then orders that 160 gold ducats of his own be put in the merchant's cart as well as one extra. When the merchant finds that the money has been returned along with an extra ducat he appears before Vlad and tells him what he has found. At the same time the thief is found and the original money returned. Vlad then orders that the thief be impaled for his crime but also tells the presumably terrified merchant that, if he had not shown such honesty and reported the one extra gold ducat, he also would have suffered execution through impalement.

Elizabeth Báthory

It has been suggested that the historical figure of Elizabeth Báthory also influenced the development of the European literary vampire. Born on 7 August 1560 in Nyirbátor in Hungary, she is today widely regarded as one of the most infamous serial killers in history. Báthory has been given lurid labels such as 'Countess Dracula' and the 'Blood Countess' by some authors. She was the daughter of George and Anna Bathory, both of whom had important aristocratic family connections in Hungary and other nearby kingdoms. Perhaps most significantly Anna was the niece of the King of Poland, Stephen Báthory, who had fought with Vlad the Impaler against the Turks and their supporters. There have even been claims that Elizabeth Báthory was related to Vlad the Impaler. She also held power in Transylvania during her lifetime, a fact that has captured the popular imagination.

Báthory married Ferenc Nádasdy in 1575 and the couple based themselves at Cachtice Castle close to the Carpathian Mountains. Nádasdy was to lead the Hungarian army into battle against the forces of the Ottoman Turks in 1578. Elizabeth Báthory took responsibility for her husband's extensive lands and holdings at various points in their marriage.

Between around 1602 and 1604, complaints about atrocities committed by Báthory came to light but they were not properly investigated at first perhaps due to fears that the nobility would be discredited. In 1611, a trial was held in which she was accused of the murder of more than 50 young girls. She refused to appear at the trial. As well as the allegations of murder, Báthory was accused of sexual abuse and torture. As a result of the trial her accomplices were punished by being beheaded or having their fingers torn off. She was walled up in a set of rooms in her castle. Food was delivered to her via a small hole in one of the walls. She was found dead in her castle on 21 August 1614.

As the mythology surrounding the murders of Elizabeth Báthory grew it began to be claimed that she had carried out the killings in order that she could both drink and bathe in the blood of her victims in a search for perpetual youth. A Jesuit scholar named László Turóczi produced a book about her called *Tragica Historia* in 1729. His version of events was the first to make the claim that she had bathed in the blood of her victims.

Chapter Four

The Vampire
in the Nineteenth Century

John Polidori

Some have argued that *The Vampyre* (1819) by John
Polidori was the first vampire story ever to be published
in English. Polidori was born on 7 September 1795 in
London. His father was the Italian scholar Gaetano
Polidori and his mother was Anna Maria Pierce who
worked as a governess. In 1810, Polidori travelled
to Scotland to train as a doctor at the University of
Edinburgh. After studying for five years, he became
a doctor of medicine in 1815. Interestingly, in view of
the later work of fiction for which he would become
famous, he chose the subject of somnambulism or sleep
walking for his degree thesis and was only 19 years old
when he qualified. The following year, Polidori became
the personal physician of the poet Lord Byron and
travelled with him to Europe. He was present at and
played an important role in one of the most celebrated
and infamous events in the history of romanticism

and in the genesis of the modern horror novel. In the summer of 1816, Lord Byron rented a house close to Lake Geneva in Switzerland called the Villa Diodati. Byron, accompanied by Polidori, stayed at the villa with Percy Bysshe Shelley and Mary Wollstonecraft Godwin. Mary's stepsister Claire Clairmont was also present at what was to prove to be a significant moment in the development of literature and popular culture.

Due to the terrible weather that Europe was experiencing that summer, Byron and his companions often found themselves confined within the walls of the villa. In fact, the weather of 1816 was so bad that it would come to be widely known as 'The Year Without a Summer'. Perhaps more revealingly in terms of the impact it had on society it was also more darkly referred to as the 'Poverty Year'. But it was not only Europe that suffered from strange climatic abnormalities that year as Eastern Canada and the Northeast of America experienced conditions that destroyed important crops. Unseasonable frosts in May 1816, followed by snowstorms and blizzard conditions in June, not only caused irreparable damage to crops but also caused fatalities amongst local populations. Bizarrely for the summer months, rivers and lakes were reported frozen in parts of America and people endured hardship and disease, and struggled with the inevitable impact of these events on food prices.

In Europe, summer rainfall was dramatically increased and there was devastating and widespread flooding which also destroyed essential crops and generally wreaked havoc amongst local populations. The resultant shortages of food led to civil unrest in Britain with rioting and attacks on warehouses containing grain. However, the worst social disruption to occur in 1816 took place in Switzerland where the shortage of food was so dire that the government proclaimed a state of national emergency. At the time the causes of these appalling and destructive weather conditions were unknown but it is now thought that they were among the consequences of a major volcanic eruption. Between the dates of 5 April and 15 April of the previous year the greatest volcanic eruptions to take place since 180 AD occurred at Mount Tambora in Indonesia. These hurled massive quantities of dust into the upper atmosphere which acted as a barrier to sunlight. The effects of the eruptions at Mount Tambora were exacerbated by the lingering effects of earlier volcanic eruptions in 1812 at La Soufriere on the Caribbean island of St Vincent and also an eruption in the Philippines that took place in 1814. Scientists today also point out that the backdrop to this volcanic activity was a period of time referred to as the Dalton Minimum when solar activity was particularly reduced. This combination of factors, as we have seen, was to have catastrophic consequences for human society. And it would provide the almost apocalyptic backdrop to the fateful meeting of Lord Byron and his guests in Switzerland in the historically significant year of 1816.

Forced by the terrible weather to stay indoors and abandon any outdoor activities, the group discussed occult themes and talked about the powers of science and particularly about the then new and potentially frightening subject of the effects of electricity.

During one particular June evening the group entertained one another by reading each other stories from a collection of macabre fiction called *Tales of the Dead* (1812).

After reading from *Tales of the Dead*, Byron famously suggested that each person present attempt to write their own ghost story which they would then later tell one another. The person who wrote the most terrifying tale would then be judged to be the winner by the group.

Mary Wollstonecraft Godwin, who would later become Mary Shelley following her marriage to Percy Bysshe Shelley, was to produce the most notable response to the challenge, a story that was to form the basis of the classic horror novel *Frankenstein*.

According to the author's introduction to the Standard Novels Edition (1831), Byron and Percy Shelley had discussed in detail 'the nature of the principle of life, and whether there was any probability of its ever being discovered and communicated' (Mary Shelley, *Frankenstein*, p8). Mary Shelley describes listening to the two men converse whilst she remained virtually silent as they hypothesised whether a corpse could be brought back to life by scientific means. The frightening subject matter of that evening's conversation fired Mary Shelley's imagination and she later described how, 'with shut eyes, but acute mental vision – I saw the pale student of unhallowed arts kneeling beside the thing he had put together. I saw the hideous phantasm of a man stretched out, and then, on the workings of some powerful engine, show signs of life, and stir with an uneasy, half-vital motion,' (Mary Shelley, *Frankenstein*, p9).

Byron himself wrote the beginnings of a ghost story but failed to complete it. 'The fragment' as it is commonly known was later to be printed at the end of his poem *Mazeppa* (1819). In Byron's story a young man relates how he meets and travels with a sophisticated and charismatic aristocrat called Augustus Darvell.

Their journey across Europe ends with a final trip to the ruins of Ephesus in Turkey where Darvell, whose health has been failing throughout the tale, finally dies in a Turkish cemetery. Before dying Darvell asks that his young companion cast his seal ring, decorated with Arabic characters, into the salt springs that run into the Bay of Eleusis a month from that date, with the implication that he will in some manner be resurrected. The brief story outline concludes with the young man and a Turkish janissary named Suleiman who has accompanied them burying Darvell. Following their stay in Switzerland, Lord Byron and John Polidori were to travel together for around five months.

Finally, Lord Byron dismissed Polidori as his physician and travelling companion after apparently growing tired of the younger man provoking arguments with him. Polidori was to continue his travels alone for a brief period but eventually made his way home to England where he practised medicine in Norwich. Polidori attempted to retrain in law and gave up his medical career but failed to finish his studies. In London, he lived on Great Pulteney Street in Soho where a blue plaque commemorating this can be seen today.

Polidori took the material that Byron had cast aside after their stay at Lake Geneva and used it as the basis for a tale of his own invention called *The Vampyre*.

It was published on 1 April 1819 in *The New Monthly Magazine*. The appearance of the story caused great controversy because the publisher of the magazine Henry Colburn credited it as 'A Tale by Lord Byron'. In fact the story was entirely written by Polidori but he had left the manuscript in Geneva and it had made its way into the hands of Colburn. In Byron's original fragment of a story the poet had clearly based the romantic figure of the aristocratic Darvell on himself and used Polidori as the model for his young companion. In an interesting reversal Polidori reshapes Darvell as the sinister and frightening figure of Lord Ruthven and bases this character on the scandalous and colourful reputation of Lord Byron and casts himself as his companion Aubrey.

In May 1816, Lady Caroline Lamb, an ex-girlfriend of Lord Byron, had produced the novel *Glenarvon* in which a character who is obviously based on Lord Byron, called Clarence de Ruthven, Lord Glenarvon, appears. The novel paints Byron as an arrogant villain and was intended by the author as an act of revenge against her former lover. In Polidori's story, we are presented with the concept of the Byronic hero combined with the folklore of the vampire for the first time. Lord Ruthven emerges as a devilish yet attractive fiend who finally marries the sister of the unfortunate

Aubrey and the tale concludes with the declaration that:

'Lord Ruthven had disappeared, and Aubrey's sister had slaked the thirst of a VAMPYRE!' (quoted in Mary Shelley, *Frankenstein*, Penguin, 2003, p265).

Polidori died on 24 August 1821, aged just 26, and there was immediate controversy as to the causes of his death. It is commonly stated that he died as a suicide after drinking prussic acid because he was suffering from depression caused by huge gambling debts. Another version of events states that Polidori was involved in a carriage accident that caused injuries to his head that finally proved fatal. However, the coroner's report of the time concluded that the young man had 'died by the visitation of God', in other words through natural causes.

Varney the Vampire

One of the most important examples of the development of the literary vampire is the Victorian gothic horror classic *Varney the Vampire*. It was most likely written by James Malcolm Rymer although some have said it was the work of Thomas Preskett Prest. Its full title on publication was *Varney the Vampire or The Feast of Blood* and it first appeared as a number of pamphlets starting in 1845 and running through to 1847. These types of pamphlets are often referred to as 'penny dreadfuls'. The description indicates their price and also gives a clue as to their often grisly and horrific contents. Perhaps because of the nature of the format in which it was originally produced, *Varney the Vampire* consists of a massive 220 chapters. Rymer was paid by his publisher for each line that he produced and its sprawling length reflects this. Although it was published in book form during 1847, its structure betrays its origins as a popular and long-running penny dreadful.

The story concerns vampiric attacks made upon the Bannerworth family by Sir Francis Varney of Ratford Hall in Yorkshire. Interestingly, Varney claims that he was cursed to become a vampire because during the English Civil War he betrayed the Royalists and then was damned for killing his own son. There are within *Varney the Vampire* a number of characteristics and ideas that have become the norm in vampire fiction and that can be found within *Dracula*. Like Stoker's vampire Sir Francis Varney bites his victims with two prominent fangs that leave a tell-tale wound on their necks. He also shares the count's ability to hypnotise his victims. However, no claims are made that he is repulsed by garlic or crucifixes. Significantly, *Varney the Vampire* contains dramatic elements that would later appear in *Dracula*. The vampire is able to change shape into that of a wolf and there is a scene that mirrors that of Van Helsing and the vampire hunters waiting expectantly at the tomb of Lucy Westenra. There is also an episode in which an empty and seemingly deserted ship appears mysteriously, much like Dracula's arrival in England at Whitby aboard the *Demeter*. Varney is also (importantly) described as a victim of his condition; he detests himself but cannot stop his behaviour. The notion of a sympathetic vampire who is disgusted by their own condition has become a common feature of the vampire genre.

Carmilla

Many have argued that the Gothic novella *Carmilla* by Sheridan Le Fanu, first published in 1872, was a major influence on Bram Stoker's novel *Dracula*.

Carmilla originally appeared within the pages of a magazine called *The Dark Blue* in its January, February and March issues of 1872. It was also published later that year in a collection of Le Fanu's short stories entitled *In a Glass Darkly*. Joseph Sheridan Le Fanu was probably the most famous writer of ghost stories of his era. He was born on 28 August 1814 at 45 Lower Dominick Street in Dublin. Although he studied law at Trinity College, Dublin Le Fanu opted instead for a career as a writer. His first ghost story called 'The Ghost and the Bone-Setter' was published in 1838 in the *Dublin University Magazine*. Le Fanu was to become the owner of the *Dublin Evening Mail* as well as a number of other newspapers.

Carmilla tells the strange tale of a wealthy Englishman who retires with his daughter Laura to live in a castle in Styria, located in the southeast of Austria. As a child Laura tells a story of how she had been visited by a beautiful visitor who had bitten her on the chest. Later on, when Laura is a young woman she is joined at the castle by a young girl called Carmilla who has been involved in a carriage accident. Laura believes she is the same beautiful stranger whom she saw biting her.

Her mother leaves Carmilla at the castle whilst she claims to undertake an important journey. Laura and Carmilla become good friends, although their relationship also involves Carmilla's amorous feelings towards Laura. Carmilla tells little about herself and also sleepwalks during the night. Laura later has dreams that she is visited by a strange creature at night that bites her and then leaves her room in the shape of a beautiful woman. Laura is then taken ill from some mysterious cause as is the niece of General Spielsdorf and it is soon realised that both girls are the victims of a vampire.

When Laura's father and the General discuss their experiences they conclude that the vampire in question is Mircalla, Countess Karnstein. The Countess has been a vampire for 200 years and adopted the names of Carmilla and Millarca, (anagrams of her own name) in order to attack Laura and the General's niece. They meet Carmilla in a ruined chapel and the General recognises her as the same young woman who attacked his niece. Finally the threat of the vampire is ended when the body of the Countess is found and the fathers destroy it.

It has been noted that Bram Stoker's earliest manuscript of *Dracula* from 1890 also sets his tale in Styria rather than the more familiar country of Transylvania that is now such a recognisable part of the vampire mythology. Interestingly, the short story 'Dracula's Guest' that was published by Stoker's widow after his death is also set in Styria and for a more detailed examination of its relationship to *Dracula* see Chapter Six. Other notable parallels between *Dracula* and *Carmilla* include their depictions of the female vampires in both stories. Carmilla is described as languid and tall in appearance and having a sensual face with full lips and large eyes. The character of

Lucy Westenra in *Dracula* who is preyed upon by the count in Whitby is also described in this way and both characters are also said to sleepwalk and to have softly spoken voices.

It has also been observed that both classic vampire tales feature an investigative doctor who realises that a vampire has been attacking people in the story. In the case of *Carmilla* this is Dr Hesselius who parallels in many ways the role of Stoker's Van Helsing. Carmilla, like Dracula, is able to change her form, in her case metamorphosing into a cat rather than a large dog like the count. She can also mysteriously pass through solid walls in much the same way Dracula can take on the form of a strange mist or glowing particles. Both vampires also sleep in a coffin.

It has been observed that Sheridan Le Fanu and Bram Stoker had much in common as both were from Anglo-Irish backgrounds and both had strongly protestant upbringings. It is interesting to note that William Le Fanu, the brother of Sheridan Le Fanu, was a Commissioner of Public Works at Dublin Castle during the same period that Bram Stoker's father was also working there as a third-class clerk in the Chief Secretary's Office. Bram Stoker himself was to work as a clerk in the Petty Sessions office at the same time as William Le Fanu's son Thomas Philip Le Fanu was also working at Dublin Castle as a first class clerk in the Chief Secretary's Office.

It has also been noted with some interest that *Carmilla* was published in a Trinity College magazine at the same time as Bram Stoker was studying there and had started to produce weird fiction of his own.

Carmilla is also significant within the evolution of the horror genre and its representation of vampires has been particularly influential on subsequent filmmakers.

The classic 1932 film *Vampyr* by the Danish director Carl Dreyer was based on the Le Fanu collection of ghost stories entitled *In A Glass Darkly* that included *Carmilla* and it draws a number of stylistic elements from the vampire tale. Perhaps most famously, *Carmilla* was adapted by Hammer Films in 1970 under the title of *The Vampire Lovers*. This starred Ingrid Pitt as Carmilla, and Hammer Films made the theme of lesbian eroticism explicit. Its success led to two further films featuring the character of Carmilla: *Lust for a Vampire* in 1971 and *Twins of Evil* in the same year.

Chapter Five

Bram Stoker

A number of commentators and biographers have observed that Bram Stoker was, in many ways, an unlikely candidate to have created one of the greatest and most enduring of all figures in horror fiction and popular culture. He was born on 8 November 1847 at Clontarf, close to the city of Dublin, and named after his father Abraham Stoker. His mother was called Charlotte Mathilda Thornley Stoker. His parents were members of the Clontarf Church of Ireland parish and had their children baptised in their local church of St John the Baptist at Seafield Road West. His father spent his whole life working as a civil servant and he was initially to play an important role in the development of Stoker's own career. His parents had a total of seven children of which Bram Stoker was the third born.

Perhaps the most dramatic aspect of his childhood was that he was bedridden until the age of seven. He was apparently suffering from an undiagnosed illness from which he eventually recovered and afterwards resumed a normal childhood. It has been observed that there are parallels between Stoker's own experience here and the fictional diaries of Jonathan Harker when he is attempting to recover from the trauma of his stay at Castle Dracula. It is interesting to note that three of Stoker's brothers studied medicine and that Stoker had a strong link to the medical world that he would later draw on whilst writing *Dracula* particularly in relation to the character of Professor Van Helsing. Another brother was to follow their father into the civil service, taking a position overseas in India.

As a young man Stoker studied at Trinity College, Dublin, from 1864 to 1870, reading literature, history, physics and mathematics. Stoker was to distinguish himself during his time at Trinity within the field of athletics where he was named University Athlete, a striking turn of events given his unusual and undiagnosed childhood malady. He also gained the position of president of a debating club called the University Philosophical Society. It is interesting to note in this context that the first paper he produced for the society was entitled 'Sensationalism in Fiction and Society'. He also served as the auditor of the College Historical Society. Stoker's time at Trinity is also notable for his admiration for and subsequent defence of the work of the American poet Walt Whitman following criticism by other students. Whitman was something of a hero for Stoker. He corresponded with him and went on to meet him later in life during a trip to America.

Upon leaving university Stoker took up a position as a civil servant in Dublin Castle following advice from his father. During his time within the civil service Stoker wrote a non-fiction book with the enjoyably prosaic title of *The Duties of Clerks of Petty Sessions in Ireland*. Although produced in 1876 it was not to be published until 1879.

Although he worked dutifully within his new role as a civil servant it rapidly became obvious that it was work that was unfulfilling to the young Stoker. He found an outlet for his other interests by writing theatre criticism for the *Dublin Evening Mail*.

He also began writing fiction and had his first short story entitled 'The Crystal Cup' published in London Society magazine in 1872. In 1875 Stoker also had three other works published in a Dublin based magazine called *The Shamrock*. They were *The Primrose Path* (a novel in serial parts), and two novellas, *Buried Treasures* and *The Chain of Destiny*.

Perhaps the most significant event of this period of Stoker's life took place in 1876 after he wrote a glowing review of a production of *Hamlet* staged in Dublin with Henry Irving in the title role. Irving was at this time an actor whose fame was rapidly growing and Stoker's praise for his production led the two to meet. Irving read the review and invited Stoker to have dinner with him at the Shelbourne Hotel. During the meeting Irving is reported to have recited Thomas Hood's poem 'The Dream of Eugene Aram' and Stoker was so greatly moved by it that he is said to have burst into a kind of emotional, hysterical fit. He was later to comment that, after meeting Irving, he felt as if 'soul had looked into soul' (Michael Holroyd, *A Strange Eventful History*, p286).

This encounter was to have dramatic long-term consequences for the civil servant as the two men struck up a friendship and were to write regularly to one another for the next couple of years. Stoker was in many respects in awe of Irving and was a huge admirer of his abilities. Their meeting was to bear unexpected fruit for the Irishman when, in 1878, Irving offered him the position of business manager of the Lyceum Theatre at Covent Garden in London. The Lyceum was owned by Irving and was something of a new direction for the actor at the time. Henry Irving had already performed for a period of seven years when he decided to take over the running of the Lyceum and was particularly well known as a Shakespearean actor. His intention was to establish a theatre that would be regarded as of national importance. He gained particular prominence as an actor playing the role of Hamlet opposite the actress Ellen Terry who took the role of Ophelia. Ellen Terry was to become a great star of the day in her own right and the pair would work together in all of the major Shakespearean roles during their careers. In offering the role of business manager to Stoker, Irving wanted to focus more fully on the creative aspects of his work.

Accepting the offer and giving up his career in the civil service, much to the horror of his mother, Stoker also married Florence Balcombe, a well-known society beauty who had previously been involved with another famous literary son of Dublin, Oscar Wilde. The couple moved to London where Stoker became Irving's business manager, a tenure that was to last for 27 years and only ended in 1905 with the actor's death. In 1879, Florence Stoker gave birth to a son on 31 December who was christened Noel Thornley Stoker and was to be the couple's only child. However, Bram Stoker was to find his new life with Irving was something of a social whirlwind and was unable to spend much time with his new family.

His new post was to prove to be very demanding as

Irving was at that time a celebrity who moved in high social circles. This meant Stoker was able to meet a fascinating and wide array of people from the London society in which he found himself. It was during this period that Stoker met the novelist Hall Caine (1853-1931) who was a bestselling author at the time. The two men became great friends and Stoker would go on to dedicate *Dracula* to him, writing, 'To My Dear Friend Hommy-Beg', a Manx expression meaning 'little Tommy' apparently bestowed by Hall Caine's grandmother who came from the Isle of Man. Hall Caine was also to provide a fascinating insight into the relationship between Bram Stoker and Sir Henry Irving when, after Stoker's death, he wrote about the subject in his obituary. He commented that: 'Much has been said of (Stoker's relation to Henry Irving), but I wonder how many were really aware of the whole depth and significance of that association. Bram seemed to give up his life to it…I say without any hesitation that never have I seen, never do I expect to see, such absorption of one man's life in the life of another,' (Bram Stoker, *The New Annotated Dracula*, Edited by Leslie S. Klinger, p37). Many have speculated that Stoker partly based the character of Dracula on that of Sir Henry Irving and it could be argued that something of the dominating and also exhausting nature of Dracula's control over characters such as Renfield, Lucy Westenra and Mina Harker can be detected in the intensity of the relationship between the two men.

Stoker was responsible for arranging the theatrical tours of Irving and his company around the country and, in 1883, he planned Irving's first visit to North America.

It was during this tour that Stoker was able to meet the poet Walt Whitman whose work he had championed at Trinity College and another personal hero, the novelist Mark Twain. As we have seen, as a young man Stoker had defended Walt Whitman's collection of poetry *Leaves of Grass* (1855) and had written to the poet praising his work. The letters that he wrote to Whitman are of interest in that it seems to show a need in Stoker for a male hero to idolise in much the same way as he was to idolise Sir Henry Irving. Stoker even went so far as to say in his letter that, 'How sweet a thing it is for a strong healthy man with a woman's eyes and a child's wishes to feel that he can speak so to a man who can be if he wishes father, brother and wife to his soul. I don't think you will laugh Walt Whitman...' (Christopher Frayling, *Nightmare: The Birth of Horror*, p71). Some have argued that Bram Stoker may have had repressed homosexual feelings which would emerge in a twisted form in his representation of the compelling and fascinating figure of Dracula who is a figure both attractive and repellent. However, by complete contrast to the liberal figure of the gay poet Walt Whitman, Sir Henry Irving was to prove a rather harsher and more conservative hero for Stoker. Indeed Irving was to speak out against the play *Salome* (1896) by Oscar Wilde and joined in the pillorying of the writer who had been amongst Stoker's friends at Trinity.

Interestingly, when the first edition of *Dracula* was published in 1897, it appeared with what was then a fashionable yellow cover. In Oscar Wilde's famous novel of 1891 *The Picture of Dorian Gray*, the character of Dorian is described as falling under the corrupting influence of 'the yellow book'. It is believed that the book that Wilde was alluding to was *A Rebours or Against the Grain* (1884) by Joris-Karl Huysmans which relates the life and experiences of a decadent Paris sensualist and was a great influence on a number of British artists of the time such as Aubrey Beardsley. Beardsley was to be the first art editor of the literary journal *The Yellow Book* that ran from 1894 to 1897 and is credited with coming up with the title of the publication. In Paris at the time it was common for decadent works such as *A Rebours* that contained themes of hedonism and debauchery to be wrapped in yellow paper in order to warn (or attract) readers as to their content.

It seems that Stoker was to some extent influenced by *The Picture of Dorian Gray* in constructing the character of Count Dracula. Famously, Count Dracula does not cast a shadow and has no reflection in a mirror and there is a discrepancy between his appearance and the fact that he has lived an unnaturally long life. The character of Dorian Gray also has a curious dual identity. He appears young in person but his portrait, hidden away from society, ages in a hideous and horrific way that reflects his sins. From surviving notes of the time it seems that Stoker may originally have conceived of his vampiric count as having a similar character to Dorian Gray but, perhaps in the wake of the 1895 trial of Oscar Wilde, had repressed this influence. Although Stoker's work at the Lyceum was time-consuming and challenging he continued to write when time allowed and had a collection of children's short stories published in 1881 entitled *Under the Sunset*. He also produced an account of Irving's tour of America called *A Glimpse of America* in 1886.

The Origins of *Dracula*

It seems likely that the genesis of *Dracula* lay in a nightmare that Stoker experienced, probably on 7 March 1890. A surviving note written on the following day records the outline of Stoker's fearful dream: 'young man goes out – sees girl one tries to kiss him not on the lips but throat. Old Count interferes – rage and fury diabolical. This man belongs to me I want him,' (Christopher Frayling, *Nightmare: The Birth of Horror*, p68). It appears to be the kernel of an idea around which the novel was constructed. This particular nightmare would eventually form the basis for the journal entry of the night of 15 May of the character Jonathan Harker, the young solicitor trapped in Count Dracula's castle. The women who attempt to kiss the young man on the throat would become the three so-called 'Brides of Dracula' who are only turned back from preying on their victim by Dracula himself. It has been argued that the notion of three sinister women was drawn from the three witches in Shakespeare's *Macbeth*. It was a play that Sir Henry Irving had produced and starred in with great success. Stoker's nightmare seems to contain anxiety concerning the voracious sexual appetites of women but also fear of a dominating male influence that it seems likely represents Irving. On a slightly more humorous level Stoker's own son Noel would later say that the plot for *Dracula* came to his father 'in a nightmarish dream after eating too much dressed crab'.

Bram Stoker first began work on *Dracula* in 1890 and was to spend the next seven years researching and rewriting it. Whilst many of the themes and ideas within *Dracula* clearly have an enduring resonance and draw on ancient themes and myths, it is also very much a product of its time. Importantly, the publication of *Dracula* in 1897 coincided with the Diamond Jubilee of Queen Victoria. It is interesting to note that Stoker who, as an Irishman, might have been expected to have had critical views of the British Empire was in fact an ardent supporter of it.

In an interview given at the time of the publication of *Dracula* when asked what he thought of the celebrations he replied: 'Everyone has been proud that the great day went off so successfully. We have had a magnificent survey of the Empire, and last week's procession brought home, as nothing else could have done, the sense of the immense variety of the Queen's dominions,' (*Dracula,* Edited by Glennis Byron p484-488).

At this point in her reign the British Empire was at its peak of power and influence. Victoria had been crowned on 20 June 1837 as the Queen of the United Kingdom of Great Britain and Ireland. From 1 May 1876 Queen Victoria had also gained the title of Empress of India. This was to be a period of huge social change in Britain with the advent of the Industrial Revolution and growing power and control over foreign dominions. The growth of urban centres such as London, Birmingham and Manchester was fuelled by industrialisation which was also accompanied by often appalling social deprivation and living conditions.

The expansion of empire was in many ways justified by a belief that Britain was a civilising influence on less developed nations and was replacing fear and superstition with scientific knowledge accompanied by Christian missionary activity. Advances in scientific knowledge and a growing understanding of the universe as exemplified by Charles Darwin's *The Origin of Species* (1859) was also matched by an upsurge in religious belief and Victorian moral values. It has been argued that in many ways this great period of social change marked something of a transition from the superstitious beliefs of the past and the arrival of a more scientific modern age. In *Dracula* it can be argued that the narrative reflects this conflict between the fears of the past as represented by the vampiric count from the medieval world of old Europe and the team of vampire hunters led by Van Helsing who use a combination of technology and knowledge (ranging from train timetables to hypnotism) to defeat this ancient monster.

The Victorian era also produced a range of literature that proved popular with the public and combined science fiction, fantasy and horror elements. The novels of HG Wells such as *The Time Machine* (1895) and *The War of the Worlds* (1898) offered troubling visions of the future with the role of science in society providing a powerful theme in his work. The threat of invasion from other countries or other worlds also emerges in Victorian literature of this time. As we have seen, *The Picture of Dorian Gray* concerns a central character with a dark secret life whose real nature is corrupt and repulsive. It has also been noted that the bestselling novel of 1894, *Trilby* by George du Maurier, with its story of a young woman who is transformed and moulded into a famous singer by an impresario called Svengali, bears comparison with *Dracula*. Svengali uses hypnotism to control his protégé and there are parallels between his relationship with Trilby and that of Dracula with his victims Mina Harker and Lucy Westenra.

The Storyline of *Dracula*

In order to better understand the themes and ideas within *Dracula* and its influence on culture since its publication it is now necessary and helpful to provide a more detailed plot outline. It is structured in the form of a series of different documents from a number of sources that relate the progress of the events that it describes. In this sense there is no single voice leading its narrative and it seems surprisingly modern even today in terms of its construction. Sources such as diary entries, newspaper clippings and letters arranged in order of their date create the book's structure.

It has been observed that this idiosyncratic approach with its methodical, carefully arranged pattern of documents is likely to have been informed by Stoker's experience as a civil servant and petty clerk.

The novel begins with the diary entry for 3 May of a young Englishman called Jonathan Harker who has recently qualified as a solicitor. He is travelling from England to visit the castle of a Transylvanian nobleman called Count Dracula.

Dracula's castle is located in the Carpathian Mountains in a district on the borders of Transylvania, Bukovina and Moldavia. Harker has been sent by his employer Peter Hawkins who is based in Exeter in

England to oversee a real estate purchase that Dracula is making in England of a property called Carfax Abbey in London. Upon arrival at Castle Dracula it soon becomes clear to Harker that there is something unusual about his host.

Although the business transaction goes ahead as planned, Harker comes to realise that he has become a prisoner in the castle. Harker later witnesses Dracula emerge from a window outside the castle at night and crawl unnaturally, face down, down the vertical wall. He soon begins to ignore the count's instructions to stay in his room at night. Harker leaves his room and searches desperately for an exit from the castle and finds himself in a room with three female vampires, the 'Brides of Dracula', who appear to put a spell on him so that he is unable to escape. However, they are prevented from drinking his blood by the arrival of Dracula who throws them back from the young English solicitor. He plans to keep Harker alive in order to gain information about London and England where he plans to travel looking for new victims to turn into vampires amongst its 'teeming millions'. Harker finally escapes the confines of the castle, deeply traumatised by what he has experienced. In July, a Russian ship called the *Demeter* sets sail from Varna and arrives in Whitby during a ferocious storm. When the ship runs aground a mysterious dog leaps ashore, according to eyewitnesses, and the entire crew are found dead with the captain lashed to the ship's wheel. The only cargo found aboard the vessel consists of boxes of earth and silver sand. The ship's log describes the strange disappearances and deaths of its crew and it becomes apparent that they have been transporting the vampire Count Dracula to England.

Wilhelmina 'Mina' Murray (who is the fiancée of Jonathan Harker) is on holiday in Whitby at the time of the *Demeter's* arrival and Dracula begins to pursue her friend Lucy Westenra. Lucy is being wooed by three young men who all propose to her on one day. The young men are an asylum psychiatrist called Dr John Seward, the Honourable Arthur Holmwood and a visiting American cowboy called Quincey P Morris. Mina sees Dracula and Lucy encounters him in St Mary's Churchyard on the cliffs above Whitby. The count transforms Lucy into a vampire by biting her and drinking her blood. Dr Seward and his friends, assisted by the enigmatic Professor Van Helsing, attempt to save her with blood transfusions using their own blood.

However, Lucy dies and is interred at Highgate Cemetery in London from where she preys on children in her undead incarnation as a vampire on Hampstead

Heath. She is destroyed by Van Helsing and his associates who drive a stake through her heart.

Mina Harker is also vampirised by Dracula and in response Van Helsing and the others methodically destroy his resting places of coffins filled with earth from his homeland. The movements of the count are tracked by a patient of Dr Seward's asylum called Renfield who craves lives to feed on. Finally, the count flees England after all his hiding places have been destroyed and the vampire slayers pursue him back to his castle in Transylvania, aided by Mina's telepathic link with him. Eventually the transportation of the count by gypsies is halted and Jonathan Harker cuts off his head with a Kukri knife whilst Quincey stabs him through the heart with his Bowie knife. Dracula's body immediately crumbles into dust and Mina is freed from his malign influence. Quincey dies from wounds inflicted in the chase and later Jonathan and Mina name their own son after him and eventually revisit Transylvania with him.

Chapter Six

The Creation of *Dracula*

Whitby

The Yorkshire town of Whitby plays a crucial and dramatic role in Dracula's arrival in England and it appears to have also been instrumental in providing Bram Stoker with inspiration for his novel. At the end of July 1890, Stoker travelled to Whitby where he spent some time in the town alone before he was joined by his wife Florence and his son Noel. They appear to have arrived around 8 August and this was reported in the *Whitby Gazette* on 15 August. A number of the key plot elements for the novel appear to have arisen from his visit. In particular, the content of chapters six to eight of *Dracula* drew on conversations that Stoker had with a number of local fishermen and coastguards.

Stoker also spent time in the churchyard of St Mary's which Mina Murray calls, 'the nicest spot in Whitby,' (Bram Stoker, *Dracula*, Penguin Classics, 2011, p.71). The church lies to the east side of the harbour and is reached by a long series of steps known as the church stairs. Stoker kept extensive notes from his visit to Whitby and it is interesting to consider that, although he had turned his back on the duties of the civil service, something of the careful and methodical habits he had gained from his work in Dublin Castle survived, and aided him in writing fiction. It was from local fishermen that Stoker picked up folklore concerning the ghost of the White Lady that was said to haunt Whitby Abbey. Of particular significance is a conversation that Stoker had with a coastguard called William Petherick. It was about a Russian schooner that had travelled from the Black Sea to Whitby and that had run into Tate Hill Pier on 24 October 1885. The wreck had drawn particular attention because the vessel called the *Dimetry* from Narva in Russia had run aground with all sails up. Its cargo had been silver sand from the mouth of the Danube.

Stoker also visited the local museum and subscription library. During his visit to the library he consulted a book entitled *An Account of the Principalities of Wallachia and Moldavia: with various political observations relating to them* by 'William Wilkinson, Esq, late British Consul Resident at Bukarest'. It was in this library book that Stoker appears to have come across a history of the life of Vlad Tepes, referred to as the Voivode Dracula. Up until this point it appears from Stoker's original notes that he had intended to call his principal character 'Count Wampyr'. Stoker took notes about the life of Vlad Tepes and also wrote down details about medieval Wallachia and the Carpathian Mountains.

Stoker actually copied a short section from page 19 of the book in its entirety that read, 'Dracula in the Wallachian language means Devil. The Wallachians were, at that time, as they are at present, used to give this as a surname to any person who rendered himself conspicuous either by courage, and actions, or cunning,' (Christopher Frayling, *Nightmare: The Birth of Horror*, p86). Stoker also researched local folklore from the Whitby area and took particular note of a belief in demons called 'barguests'. A barguest was said locally to be able to take different shapes including that of a terrifying dog with burning eyes. It was also said that those who heard the shrieks of the barguest at night were soon to die. Although Stoker drew a great deal of inspiration for *Dracula* from his holidays in Whitby it seems that he was also influenced by visits to the coast of northeast Scotland. In August 1893, he visited Peterhead and whilst out walking came upon the small fishing village of Port Erroll which is today known as Cruden Bay. By his own description he fell in love with the place and is thought to have been inspired by visits to nearby Slains Castle, perched dramatically on top of cliffs north of Cruden Bay, when describing Castle Dracula in his novel.

Stoker may also have been inspired in writing *Dracula* by real events concerning the Pre-Raphaelite poet Dante Gabriel Rossetti and his wife Elizabeth Siddal. Interestingly, Rossetti was the nephew of Dr John Polidori who wrote *The Vampyre* (see Chapter Four). When Elizabeth Siddal died in 1862 she was buried in the Rossetti family tomb at Highgate Cemetery along with a book of love poems written by the poet. However, Rossetti later decided that he wanted the poems back and wished to publish them. He gained permission to exhume the body. Upon opening the coffin it was said that the body of Elizabeth Siddal was in an incredible state of preservation and, it was claimed, was briefly surrounded by an unusual halo. Stoker knew Rossetti personally as well as being best friends with his later biographer the novelist Hall Caine to whom *Dracula* is dedicated. It is likely that this story provided the basis for the staking of the vampiric Lucy Westenra in *Dracula* although Stoker portrays her not as mystical or angelic but as sexual, predatory and evil.

A number of authors have commented upon the

similarity of Bram Stoker's description of the appearance of his fictional character Count Dracula and surviving contemporary observations of his historical namesake Vlad Dracula, as described in Chapter Three. However, there appear also to be physical similarities between the fictional count and Stoker's employer Sir Henry Irving whose performances were for many very melodramatic and involved much wild gesticulation and shouting.

Bram Stoker gives a detailed description of the physical appearance of Dracula as a means to also illustrate something of the character of the man.

'His face was a strong, a very strong, aquiline, with high bridge of the thin nose and peculiarly arched nostrils; with lofty domed forehead, and hair growing scantily round the temples, but profusely elsewhere. His eyebrows were very massive, almost meeting over the nose, and with bushy hair that seemed to curl in its own profusion. The mouth, so far as I could see it under the heavy moustache, was fixed and rather cruel-looking, with peculiarly sharp white teeth; these protruded over the lips, whose remarkable ruddiness showed astonishing vitality in a man of his years. For the rest, his ears were pale and at the tops extremely pointed; the chin was broad and strong, and the cheeks firm though thin. The general effect was one of extraordinary pallor.' Jonathan Harker's Journal, 5 May. (Bram Stoker, *Dracula*, Penguin Classics, 2011, p24).

It has been argued that one of the reasons why *Dracula* works so effectively as a horror story and succeeds in building tension as a novel is due to its epistolary structure. The narrative is constructed by carefully arranging together a series of documents that includes diary entries, newspaper cuttings, business letters and other sources. This structuring technique means that the reader is themselves piecing together the events and making sense of them and this heightens the sense of dread experienced through the unfolding events. It is ironic that, in producing such an effective narrative form for creating fear and building suspense, Stoker was drawing on his own altogether more humdrum experiences as a civil servant in Ireland where he was expected to piece together often dry material with an eye for detail. Stoker was also influenced in structuring *Dracula* by *The Woman in White* by Wilkie Collins which was published in 1860. Like *Dracula* it is an epistolary novel and was hugely popular during the nineteenth century. However, by the time that *Dracula* was published in 1897, this narrative form was clearly no longer particularly unusual.

The Land Beyond The Forest

Whilst Stoker was able to draw on his experiences in Britain in writing *Dracula*, he never actually travelled in Eastern Europe and Transylvania where much of the story takes place. Instead he drew much of the background material from visits to the circular reading room of the British Museum. It is ironic that arguably the most vivid and well-remembered section of the novel was constructed through careful reading and research rather than direct experience. As mentioned previously, Stoker originally intended to set *Dracula* in Styria (now part of Austria) which was the setting for the famous vampire tale *Carmilla* by fellow Irish writer Sheridan Le Fanu (see Chapter Four). However, during his research he decided to set his story in Transylvania. Particularly important to the making of this decision was his reading of *The Land Beyond the Forest* (1888) by Emily Gerard.

The name Transylvania translates as 'the land beyond the forest' and Gerard, who was married to an officer in the Austro-Hungarian cavalry, recorded in considerable detail in her book many of the superstitions and folklore of the country.

Stoker was also to utilise the maps and research material in a book entitled *Transylvania: its products and its people* (1865) by Charles Boner. Stoker appears to have drawn many details that would find their way into *Dracula* from these and other books such as *Round About the Carpathians* (1878) by Andrew Crosse. Interestingly Crosse describes how he carried a bowie knife on his travels, the same type of knife with which Dracula is stabbed through the heart by Quincey Morris at the novel's climax. It seems also that certain details described by Jonathan Harker at the beginning of *Dracula* concerning his journeys through Transylvania, such as the recipe for paprika hendl, a chicken dish seasoned with paprika, were taken from Crosse's book.

Another key work on which Stoker appears to have drawn was *On the Track of the Crescent: Erratic notes from the Piraeus to Pesth* (1885) by Major EC Johnson who described the reverence with which local people regarded roadside crosses in Transylvania, an observation that found its way into Harker's famous coach journey through the forest and mountains of Dracula's native land. Stoker's background research also included *The Book of Were-Wolves* (1865) by the Reverend Sabine Baring-Gould. He drew heavily on material from this book in describing wolves living in the Carpathian Mountains and the mysterious dog into which Dracula transforms himself. As well as reading about the real life figure of Vlad Tepes, in the reference library at Whitby, Stoker probably also saw medieval pamphlets about his life in the British Museum. However, Stoker makes his character a count as opposed to a voivode or prince like the real-life Vlad Dracula.

The term count describes a foreign nobleman whose status corresponds to that of an English earl. He also locates the castle of his fictional character close to the Borgo Pass on the border of Transylvania as opposed to the castle at Poenari built by Vlad Tepes near to Curtea de Argeş. He also does not mention Vlad's famous use of impalement as a punishment so it seems likely that Stoker only used certain details from his life. In fact, he may have merged information from Vlad Tepes's reign and that of his father Vlad II in order to build his story. It is interesting to note that in the novel Dracula describes himself as being from a Székely racial background but Vlad Tepes was an ethnic Vlach.

Arminius Vámbéry

It has been argued that the character of Van Helsing was partly based on the real-life figure of Arminius

Vámbéry. He was a well-known Hungarian traveller and scholar who knew Bram Stoker and who, some claim, advised Stoker on aspects of Transylvanian culture. Most famously in Chapter Twenty Three of *Dracula* in the 3 October entry of Dr Seward's diary, the doctor writes of the count, 'As I have learned from the researches of my friend Arminius of Buda-Pesth, he was in life a most wonderful man' (Bram Stoker, *Dracula*, Penguin Classics, 2011, p321).

Vámbéry was born on 19 March 1832 in Szentgyorgy which was then in Hungary and was from a poor Jewish background. He was originally known as Hermann Bamberger but adopted a number of aliases in his life, the best known of which was Arminius Vámbéry. Vámbéry suffered from a serious limp and was short in stature. He is said to have shown an aptitude for linguistics at a very young age but had unfortunately left school prematurely because of family money problems.

However, when he became the tutor of the village innkeeper, he was assisted by friends to gain further education himself. He went on to study in what is today Bratislava and also in the cities of Vienna and Budapest. Vámbéry was to excel in languages and was able to speak Latin, French, German, English, Hungarian and a number of other Eastern European languages as a teenager.

At the age of 20 he travelled to Istanbul where he took up a position as a private tutor in the house of Pasha Huseyin Daim teaching European languages. Vámbéry had a particular fascination and interest in the history and culture of the Ottoman Empire and was able to speak Turkish. He went on to serve as secretary to Fuat Pasha. He became best known in Western Europe as a daring traveller after he undertook a journey in 1861 from Istanbul to central Asia. He was by now fluent in, it is claimed, around 20 different Ottoman languages and had been elected as a member of the Hungarian Academy of Sciences who funded his, for the time, unusual journey. He travelled in disguise as a member of a group of travelling Dervishes and hid his true identity by adopting the name of Reshit Efendi. His journey took him to Trebizond then on to Persia and Iran. From Khiva in central Asia Vámbéry travelled on to Samarkand. He was in a potentially dangerous situation in Samarkand when he was summoned for a personal audience before its ruler who, it seems, had doubts about his actual identity. However, he was allowed to leave with gifts and travelled back to Istanbul, arriving there in March 1863.

When he travelled back to Europe in 1864, news of his daring and dangerous journey made him famous, as he was the first contemporary Westerner to travel in this way in these Eastern regions. He went on to produce a book that year about his experiences entitled *Travels in Central Asia*. He also gave sell-out lecture tours to audiences fascinated by his colourful experiences in foreign lands. Bram Stoker first encountered Vámbéry in April 1889 when he was staying at Sandringham with Sir Henry Irving as a guest of the Prince of Wales.

When Stoker published a biography of Irving in 1906 he included an entire chapter on Arminius Vámbéry. Many believe that he and Stoker had conversations about Vámbéry's home country of Hungary. He also seems likely to have given Stoker the titles of a number of books that would be of assistance to him researching the background to *Dracula*.

In 1865 the University of Budapest in Hungary gave Vámbéry the position of professor of Oriental languages. One hundred and forty years later, it emerged that he had worked for the British Government as a spy. He was known during his lifetime for defending English foreign policy in Central Asia and often spoke out about Russian expansionism and influence in the region. His role as a spy was to protect British interests in central Asia against the Russians. He was also well known in his lifetime for proposing the theory that the languages of Hungary and Turkish were in fact connected. He put forward the proposition that both had roots in North Asia. This caused great controversy at the time but modern linguists recognise that there are strong similarities between them although the exact reasons for this are still debated.

The Publication of *Dracula*

Bram Stoker had originally intended to give his vampire story the title *Count Wampyr* but he changed his mind and decided to call it *The Undead*. However, shortly before its publication, he changed the title again to *Dracula*. It had an initial print run of 3,000 copies and was sold at a price of 6 shillings by the publisher, Archibald Constable and Company. *Dracula* was published in May 1897. Stoker held a copyright reading of the novel at the Lyceum Theatre on 18 May of that year. It has been argued that Stoker partly based the character of Dracula on his mentor and employer Sir Henry Irving and it seems likely that he had hoped Irving would play the count himself. He was to be cruelly disappointed as the actor refused to take part in the reading at all. Instead a Mr Jones is reported to have played the part of the count with Ellen Terry's daughter Edith in the role of Mina Harker. When

Stoker asked Irving what he had thought of the reading he is said to have replied loudly, 'Dreadful!' Quite why he gave such a rude reaction to the reading has been the source of some debate.

It is, of course, possible that he simply did not like the material but it has been suggested that he wanted to keep Stoker in his position of business manager of the Lyceum Theatre, and did not want to encourage him to follow the career path of a writer. However, the author Michael Holroyd has observed that, 'the irony is that, had he foreseen the extraordinary success of Stoker's horror story, he might have revived the (then) ebbing fortunes of the Lyceum at the turn of the century.' (Michael Holroyd, *A Strange Eventful History*, p287).

Despite Irving's criticisms, *Dracula* generally received good reviews on its initial publication. In the *Daily Mail* review of the novel printed on 1 June 1897 it was observed that: 'In seeking a parallel to this weird, powerful and horrorful story our mind reverts to such tales as *The Mysteries of Udolpho*, *Frankenstein*, *The Fall of the House of Usher*...but *Dracula* is even more appalling in its gloomy fascination than any of these,' (quoted in Nina Auerbach and David Skal, editors, *Dracula*, Norton Critical Edition, 1997, p363-364). It is interesting and perhaps slightly amusing to note that the *Times* review of 23 August 1897 warned readers that, 'We would not...recommend it to nervous persons for evening reading' (Leslie S Klinger, *The New Annotated Dracula*, p23).

Sir Arthur Conan Doyle, the celebrated author and creator of Sherlock Holmes, had high praise for *Dracula*, 'I think it is the very best story of *diablerie* which I have read for many years. It is really wonderful how with so much exciting interest over so long a book there is never an anti-climax'. Bram Stoker's own mother Charlotte Stoker wrote enthusiastically in a letter to her son concerning *Dracula* that, 'It is splendid. No book since Mrs Shelley's *Frankenstein* or indeed any other at all has come near yours in originality, or terror'. *Dracula* also enjoyed good reviews when it was published in America in 1899.

Although today *Dracula* is viewed as a literary classic and the book received enthusiastic reviews upon its publication, Stoker was never to make a great deal of money from the novel in his own lifetime. However, Stoker continued to produce fiction and remained in his post at the Lyceum Theatre. Indeed, the author had also had two other novels published shortly before the appearance of *Dracula*.

They were *The Watter's Mou* (1895) and *The Shoulder of Shasta*, published the same year. *The Watter's Mou*, like *Dracula*, drew on locations that Stoker had travelled to on family holidays, in this case Cruden Bay on the east coast of Scotland. *The Shoulder of Shasta* was set in America where Stoker had previously travelled on tour with Sir Henry Irving and the cast and staff of the Lyceum Theatre.

In 1898, he had a romantic novel called *Miss Betty* published, followed by *The Mystery of the Sea* in 1902. *The Mystery of the Sea* was again set in Cruden Bay in Scotland. The following year he produced *The Jewel of Seven Stars*, a weird tale based on ancient Egyptian themes. In April 1901, *Dracula* was reissued as an abridged sixpenny paperback edition with a yellow jacket that is of interest in that it featured an illustration personally approved by Bram Stoker. The image depicts the character of Dracula as an older man with white hair and a moustache clambering head first down the walls of Castle Dracula with a cloak that resembles the wings of a bat and with large animalistic feet and hands. He is being watched with a mixture of shock and horror by Jonathan Harker.

In 1906, Stoker enjoyed critical and popular success with his *Personal Reminiscences of Sir Henry Irving*. This account of his life working for Irving was published in two volumes and was published following the death of the actor in September 1905. Stoker was to suffer a stroke after the death of Irving that left him unconscious for 24 hours and affected his sight and walking but, if anything, he produced more work in its aftermath than he had in previous years. He had also had *The Man* published in 1905 and produced another romance in 1908 called *Lady Athlyne*. This was followed in 1908 by a collection of short stories called *Snowbound: The Record of a Theatrical Touring Party*. The following year Stoker was to return to the theme of vampires in *The Lady of the Shroud*. However, on this occasion, the tale revolves around a woman who is claimed to be a vampire but is not.

Perhaps Stoker's best-known work other than *Dracula* is the bizarre tale called *The Lair of the White Worm*, published in 1911 and made better known to modern audiences by the film adaptation of the same name by maverick director Ken Russell in 1988. By complete contrast, in 1910 Stoker published a book called *Famous Imposters* which is a collection of non-fiction stories about eccentric and strange individuals who had made fraudulent claims about themselves. Although Stoker remained active as an author, he was largely unsuccessful financially and he suffered from declining health. After suffering from a number of strokes Stoker died on 20 April 1912 aged 64 at his home at 26 St George's Square in London.

His death certificate gave the cause of death as exhaustion. However, it has been claimed that Stoker actually died from tertiary syphilis and that the cause of death given on his death certificate was something of a polite euphemism. After his death his body was cremated at Golders Green Crematorium where his ashes were placed on display in an urn. When his son Noel died in 1961, he too was cremated and his ashes placed in the urn.

'Dracula's Guest'

Whilst many people are familiar with Bram Stoker's novel *Dracula* far fewer will be aware of the associated short story 'Dracula's Guest'. This fascinating but curious work was published in 1914 by Stoker's widow Florence in a volume entitled *Dracula's Guest and Other Weird Stories*. Many of the short stories included in the collection had been previously published by magazines during Bram Stoker's lifetime. In the preface to the collection of short stories Florence Stoker wrote that, 'I have added an hitherto unpublished episode from *Dracula*. It was originally excised owing to the length of the book, and may prove of interest to the many readers of what is considered my husband's most remarkable work' (Bram Stoker, *Dracula's Guest and Other Weird Stories*, p371).

It was generally believed that 'Dracula's Guest' was in fact the original opening chapter of *Dracula* but that subsequently Stoker decided to abandon it, presumably feeling that the novel worked better without it. However, it can be argued that 'Dracula's Guest' is so different in style from *Dracula* that it is an entirely separate short story, developed from Stoker's ideas for the beginning of *Dracula*. Most notably 'Dracula's Guest' features a fairly traditional first-person narrative that is at odds with the inventive and striking approach Stoker took with *Dracula*, structuring it as he did through a series of related documents that include diary entries and newspaper reports.

The story concerns an Englishman staying in Munich who is anxious to explore the local area. The name of this character is not given but it is generally believed to be Jonathan Harker, travelling to meet Count Dracula at his home in Transylvania.

The Englishman leaves his hotel in a coach to go on a drive in the local countryside but is warned by the *maître d'hôtel*, Herr Delbruck, that he should return before nightfall because he predicts that there is going to be a storm. He also adds ominously that it is Walpurgis Night when local people believe that evil creatures and demons walk the earth freely. The Englishman dismisses such talk as nonsense and, during the carriage ride, insists that the coachmen take him to visit an abandoned village. The coachmen refuse, claiming that it is the home of undead vampires.

Following an argument, the Englishman leaves the safety of the coach and walks to the village. He sees a strange, thin, tall man in the distance who makes the horses pulling the returning coach panic and scream in terror. He carries on and, reaching the village, finds a graveyard with a huge marble tomb with the name Countess Dolingen of Gratz inscribed on it who was apparently a suicide. He observes that the tomb has had a great iron spike thrust through it. The predicted storm begins and he seeks shelter within the tomb.

On entering he is horrified to find a female vampire within but, just as he sees her, a mysterious hand hurls him back outside. The female vampire appears to be destroyed by a bolt of lightning that strikes the spike and travels into the tomb. He passes out but awakes only to find a great wolf lying on top of him licking his throat and he feels frozen in a state of semi-lethargy. The description of the wolf has striking parallels to that of Count Dracula himself, 'Its sharp white teeth gleamed in the gaping red mouth, and I could feel its hot breath fierce and acrid upon me.' (Bram Stoker, 'Dracula's Guest', p13).

Finally, soldiers sent to rescue the Englishman by Herr Delbruck from the hotel drive off the wolf. They carry him back to the city where he finds a telegram from Count Dracula has arrived at the hotel. It contains a cryptic warning that the Englishman should be protected from the dangers of wolves and snow. The Englishman concludes that he was saved because the soldiers were prompted by the telegram from the distant count. There are similarities between this encounter with the wolf and the appearance of the three female vampires in *Dracula*. Just as Jonathan Harker feels trapped in a state of ecstasy by the vampires and watches them through his eyelashes, so the character in 'Dracula's Guest' observes the wolf in a mixture of horror and arousal.

It is implied within the story that Dracula has transformed himself into the shape of a wolf, lending the whole curious incident an aura of implied homo-eroticism.

Chapter Seven

Dracula and the Development of Cinema

Whilst Bram Stoker's novel enjoyed some success following its publication, it is within the medium of cinema that his character has taken on a lasting global, iconic status. According to the Internet Movie Database the number of films that contain a reference to Dracula may rank as high as 649. It is also claimed that more than 200 films have been made that feature Count Dracula. In fact, he is second in popularity only to that other enduring product of Victorian fiction, Sherlock Holmes. In this chapter I intend to provide an overview of some of the highlights of *Dracula*'s influence on the development of cinema in the twentieth century.

Nosferatu
The classic German Expressionist silent film *Nosferatu* is often credited with being the first ever vampire film. However, some have argued that *Le Manoir du Diable* made by George Méliès in 1896 should take that

accolade. Another cinematic precursor to *Nosferatu* would be a Swedish film called *Vampyr*, produced in 1912, of which sadly no copies survive. Nonetheless, *Nosferatu* today occupies an important role in film history and is seen as the earliest surviving adaptation of *Dracula* and cinematic interpretation of the vampire story. The film was directed by FW Murnau in 1921 and released the next year under the full title of *Nosferatu: eine Symphonie des Grauens* which translates as *Nosferatu: A Symphony of Horror.*

The screenplay of the film was written by Henrik Galeen and was based on Bram Stoker's novel. However, the filmmakers did not obtain permission from Stoker's widow Florence Stoker to adapt her husband's novel. Interestingly, Murnau had also filmed a version of *The Strange Case of Dr Jekyll and Mr Hyde* (1920) by Robert Louis Stevenson with Conrad Veidt starring in both parts. Just as with Bram Stoker's *Dracula* he had failed to seek permission to film the story and retitled it as *Der Januskopf.* Although the makers of *Nosferatu* went to some lengths to change the names of characters and locations, the film was clearly based on *Dracula* and Florence Stoker successfully sued Prana Films, who produced the movie, for copyright infringement. It was to be the first and last film made by Prana who were bankrupted by the case brought by

Stoker's widow. The court ordered that prints of the film be destroyed but happily, because it had already undergone a worldwide release, some survived.

Whilst the narrative broadly follows that of Bram Stoker's novel, the film makes some striking innovations that would go on to influence many further adaptations of the Dracula story. In *Nosferatu* the central character of the vampire is named Count Orlok and is played with chilling intensity by the actor Max Schreck. Many people have observed that the word 'Schreck' in German means 'terror' and there have been a number of unlikely conspiracy style theories that the vampire was actually played by the film's director FW Murnau.

The film makes an interesting reference to the mythology and folklore of vampires by renaming the schooner *Demeter* that carries the count and his cargo of earth-filled coffins as the *Empusa*. The Empusa, as we have seen in Chapter One, were the vampiric daughters of the goddess Hecate in Greek mythology. *Nosferatu* makes a major innovation in its adaptation of *Dracula* by associating the arrival of the vampire with the coming of plague. Whereas Bram Stoker has the count travel mainly by sea from his home country of Transylvania and then arrive dramatically in the port of Whitby in a howling gale, Murnau and his collaborators transfer the action to the fictional city of Wisborg which is based on the actual German city of Wismar where some of the filming for Nosferatu took place. Just as in Bram Stoker's original story, the crew of the schooner all die horribly because of the presence of their strange passenger but, in *Nosferatu*, it is implied that the coffins filled with earth and the rats that accompany the count have transmitted the plague to them.

There is a stark contrast between the depiction of the *Demeter*, charging with all sails raised into Whitby harbour in a terrible and supernaturally driven storm controlled by the count, and the ghostly and silent arrival of the *Empusa* at Wisborg. This is a very striking section within the film as the ship glides eerily into the screen from the right of frame without any crew members in sight and the mast and sail of the ship symbolically block out the silhouette of the city's cathedral in the distance. The notion of the arrival of plague in a European city in this way would have had particular resonance to audiences at the time because, only a few years earlier in 1919, Europe had undergone a massive influenza pandemic. The severity of this was such that some have estimated that influenza may have claimed more victims than the First World War.

The striking and haunting imagery of *Nosferatu* is thought to have been greatly influenced by a number of painters whose work the filmmakers drew upon in telling the story of *Dracula*. Perhaps most strikingly the film's central image of the monstrous count crouching beside the supine figure of the female heroine Ellen appears to echo the famous gothic painting of 1781 entitled *The Nightmare* by Henry Fuseli. Comparison between the two images show startling similarities and it seems likely that the animalistic rat-like features of Count Orlok were inspired by the demon featured in this painting. In contrast to Bram Stoker's novel where Dracula is first depicted as an unpleasant, repugnant figure who becomes more attractive and elegant as the novel progresses, Count Orlok remains closer to folkloric descriptions of the vampire with an appearance more like that of a corpse-like zombie than a charming aristocrat. Other key scenes from *Nosferatu* seem to have been strongly influenced by the painter Caspar David Friedrich in imagining the settings of the film. Unusually for a German Expressionist film of this period *Nosferatu* was shot outside the confines of a film studio and features a range of real places and exteriors. Murnau drew on the work of Friedrich in composing many of his landscapes, particularly paintings such as *Morning* (1820), *Wanderer Above the Sea of Fog* (1818) and *Winter Landscape with Church* (1811).

Since its release in 1922 *Nosferatu* has created a template that other horror filmmakers have used and has been a direct influence on later interpretations of the Dracula story. The use of shadow is particularly striking perhaps most notably when the vampire is climbing the stairs to the bedroom of the heroine and his long talon-like claws are thrown in relief across the wall. The film has sparked considerable debate over the years as to its meaning and symbolism and has provided almost limitless possibilities in terms of its potential interpretation. In the infamous book *Hollywood Babylon*, author Kenneth Anger argued for a homo-erotic reading of the film whilst others have seen in the dramatic arrival in Germany of the sinister Count Orlok a yearning for the arrival of a Hitler-type figure. The hook-nosed features of the count have suggested to some that the film is anti-Semitic and that the vampire is a horrific metaphor for the attitudes to Jews in Europe.

Bela Lugosi

For many people the definitive film version of Bram Stoker's novel is the 1931 Universal Studios production of *Dracula*, starring the legendary Bela Lugosi and directed by Tod Browning. Unlike FW Murnau's silent production of *Nosferatu*, the Universal version of *Dracula* was made with the permission of Bram Stoker's widow Florence. Inspired by the success of *The Phantom of the Opera* (1925) and *The Hunchback of Notre Dame* (1923), the film's producer Carl Laemmle Jr believed that a new film adaptation of the Dracula story would prove popular with film audiences. Laemmle wanted to cast the actor Lon Chaney as the count but these plans were dashed when Chaney died of throat cancer.

The classic Universal film of *Dracula* was based on a stage adaptation of Stoker's novel produced in 1924 by the writers Hamilton Deane and John L Balderston. The circumstances around the creation of the film were troubled in several ways as the loss of Chaney in the title role also coincided with financial difficulties caused by the economic upheavals of the American Depression. Although Bela Lugosi had played the part of Dracula in the stage play by Deane and Balderston, and received good reviews for his performance, he was far from the first choice of the film studio. Several other actors, including Paul Muni, were considered for the part before the studio finally accepted Lugosi. It was widely reported that, during the making of the film, its director Tod Browning allowed the film to descend into near chaos, and was unhappy at the loss of his original choice of Lon Chaney and with the content of the script. Cinematographer Karl Freund apparently played a major role in the organisation and shooting of the film.

The success of Dracula led to a large number of horror film productions by Universal. Their adaptation of *Frankenstein* starring Boris Karloff as the monster was also released in 1931 and was followed by films such as *The Mummy* (1932), *The Invisible Man* (1933), *Bride of Frankenstein* (1935) and *The Wolf Man* (1941). The Universal film adaptation of Deane and Balderston's play differs in many respects from Bram Stoker's novel and arguably served to establish many of the conventions regarding vampires with which audiences are familiar. This film version simplifies Stoker's plethora of characters and informational sources in order to make the narrative more straightforward and comprehensible. The film opens with Renfield as the estate agent travelling to Transylvania to meet the count on Walpurgis Night, as previously noted, and not on the eve of St George's night as is the case in the novel. Upon arriving at Castle Dracula he is vampirised by Dracula and becomes his servant. He accompanies the count on his sea voyage aboard a ship called the *Vesta* rather than the *Demeter* that arrives in

Whitby with the dead captain at the ship's wheel.

Unlike *Nosferatu* the Universal version of *Dracula* is predominantly set-bound and follows many of the conventions of the play, finally excluding the frantic race across Europe for a rather swift dispatching of the count by Van Helsing in his box of earth at Carfax Abbey. The film is perhaps most remarkable for Lugosi's central performance and its eerie silences which are also a feature of the director Tod Browning's other work. Lugosi brings to his version of the count a mesmeric stare that draws on the stage performances of hypnotists that shocked and excited audiences during the Victorian era. Indeed, the theme of hypnotism within the film is a powerful one as Dracula hypnotises his victims to stop them escaping from his bloodthirsty advances and to do his bidding. After being bitten by Dracula, Mina Harker also develops a wide-eyed hypnotic stare that she attempts to use on her fiancé Jonathan Harker.

She is stopped from biting him by Van Helsing who leaps forward and brandishes a crucifix in front of her, thus establishing a convention that is widely known today. In Stoker's original novel a greater emphasis is given to charms such as garlic flowers and Holy Communion wafers which have the power to repel vampires.

Many of the lines from the film such as 'I am Dracula, I bid you welcome!' have also come to define popular representations of Dracula as has Lugosi's naturally accented performance and his slowly moving, melodramatic physical manner complete with claw-like hand gestures. The film also establishes the convention that Dracula wears a cape and this was to become forever linked in the popular imagination with Lugosi.

Lugosi's performance terrified film audiences of the time and, in many ways, crystallised what is arguably the most recognisable popular identity of the Dracula character. For Lugosi this would ultimately mean typecasting that would effectively destroy his career. Today, like the character of Dracula, Lugosi is himself a figure that fascinates people and his own life story has been the subject of film adaptations. He was born in around 1882 in what is today Lugoj in the Banat region of Romania but which was, at the time, part of Austria-Hungary.

His father was a banker called István Blaskó and his mother was called Paula de Vojnich. Lugosi came from a Roman Catholic family and began acting in Hungary, playing roles in Shakespeare plays and other productions. Before leaving Hungary, Lugosi appeared in a number of silent film roles using the name of

Arisztid Olt. He worked in films in Hungary during the period when it was controlled by Bela Kun but, after the Hungarian Soviet Republic fell in 1919, he left to find work in Germany. Whilst living in Germany, Lugosi appeared in a number of successful German film productions but finally left to travel to America in 1920. He initially arrived in the United States as an illegal immigrant at New Orleans in December of that year. However, he later underwent an official reception to the country in March 1921 when he was 'met' at Ellis Island in New York.

Bela Lugosi died on 16 August 1956 of a heart attack whilst at home in Los Angeles. There is a common belief that he asked to be buried in the cape that he wore as Dracula but this appears to be inaccurate. It was decided by his son Bela Lugosi Jr and his fifth wife Lilian that he should be buried in one of the capes that he had worn during the stage production of *Dracula*.

Hammer Films

In 1958, Hammer Films produced their version of *Dracula* starring Christopher Lee in the title role and featuring Peter Cushing as his nemesis Professor Van Helsing. Directed by Terence Fisher the film was released as *Dracula* in Britain but was known as *Horror of Dracula* in the United States of America. This was because it was thought confusion might arise between the 1931 *Dracula* with Bela Lugosi in the lead role and the Hammer film. Terence Fisher's version of the story deviates in a number of respects from the Bram Stoker novel and from the Universal movie. Arguably, Lee is even more iconic as the count than Lugosi and furthers the concept of Dracula as a charming and attractive European aristocrat who proves fatally irresistible to women.

Director Terence Fisher had achieved success for Hammer with the 1957 film *The Curse of Frankenstein*, an adaptation of the Mary Shelley novel. Many critics of the time had been outraged by the bloody style that the film adopted and it had gained Hammer films something of a reputation for gore. The Hammer adaptation of *Dracula* seems to build on this reputation from the very beginning of its title sequence where, famously, a camera tracks towards a stone sarcophagus that bears the name of the vampiric count and suddenly a shower of bright red blood covers the infamous name. In this version, the character of Jonathan Harker is a librarian not an estate agent and he arrives at Dracula's castle planning to destroy the count. Whilst Harker succeeds in killing one of the

'Brides of Dracula', he is himself vampirised. Van Helsing, played by the brilliant Peter Cushing, drives a stake through Harker's heart and later destroys his fiancée Lucy who has also become a vampire. Dracula then kidnaps the character of Mina who, in this story line, is Lucy's sister-in-law.

The film is dominated by Christopher Lee's performance as the undead count, although it is interesting to note that he has only around 13 lines of dialogue to speak throughout its running time. Instead his imposing physical stature and his ability to convey at times a detached icy coolness, as well as the kind of raging fury envisaged by Stoker in his original story, make his performance memorably compelling. His dramatic entrance at the beginning of the film, appearing, seemingly without a sound, at the top of a staircase, is a particularly powerful introduction to Lee's Dracula.

The finale of the film is also particularly inventive and innovative as Van Helsing and Dracula fight one another through the castle. In an inspired reaction that cements the significance of the crucifix in vampire cinema, Van Helsing drives Dracula off by grabbing two large candlestick holders and making the sign of the cross in the face of his famous adversary. Finally, he destroys the count by sprinting across a table top in the castle library and, leaping into the air, tearing down the closed curtains at the window. This allows the sunlight to stream in, and, in a sequence that shocked and thrilled audiences of the time, Dracula literally disintegrates into dust as his unnaturally long life finally catches up with him. However, this graphic and disturbing scene is also touched with a sense of compassion and sympathy for Dracula's wretched plight. Peter Cushing's character watches with a look of horror and sadness and perhaps a sense of pity.

Some have argued that Terence Fisher's adaptation of the Dracula story has a slightly more complex moral vision than some other versions. In some ways, it is Van Helsing who behaves like a driven, maniacal madman, hunting his quarry relentlessly and then wreaking destruction upon him. Lee commented in his autobiography that 'In my mind Dracula, the Mummy and Frankenstein's monster are driven figures, unable to help themselves, eventually out of control like a runaway train, and consequently very much alone. Audiences are terrified – very well, but they should also see the pathos of it.' (Christopher Lee, *Lord of Misrule*, p300).

In the 1960 film *Brides of Dracula*, Hammer traded on the name and reputation of Stoker's character but he remains absent from the subsequent proceedings.

Finally, in 1966 Christopher Lee reprised his famous role in the Hammer production *Dracula: Prince of Darkness*. The film features four English holidaymakers who find themselves, unwisely but through necessity, staying the night at Castle Dracula.

The plot pivots on the presence of a never-before-mentioned manservant to the count called Klove who kills Alan one of the English visitors. Klove then enacts a diabolical ritual in which the blood of his victim is poured over the ashes of Dracula who was, of course, destroyed by Van Helsing in the first Hammer film. Demonically revived by this ceremony, Dracula proceeds to terrorise the other visitors, turning Alan's wife Helen into a vampire. Christopher Lee in this film battles Andrew Keir as Father Shandor. In *Dracula: Prince of Darkness* the count is thwarted by the vampire hunters as he falls through the ice covering his own moat and is consigned to a watery grave. Many critics have observed that Lee's talents were distinctly underused, as the vampiric aristocrat who had survived for centuries in Bram Stoker's original is given relatively short shrift in this underwhelming but enjoyable sequel.

The popularity of the character as played by Lee proved such that, in 1968, Hammer resurrected him again in the self-explanatorily named *Dracula Has Risen*

From The Grave. This time Dracula is brought back to life when, a year on from the events of *Dracula: Prince of Darkness*, a Monsignor who visits his castle performs an exorcism. The film was a hit and combined strong implied sexual imagery with a sometimes psychedelic style that captured the imagination of audiences of the time.

Trashy and vulgar, the film relishes in using Christian imagery whilst breaking some of the 'rules' of the vampire genre. In one sequence for example Dracula is staked through the heart but is not destroyed because the act was not accompanied by the right prayers.

Lee has, quite understandably, been linked with the character throughout his memorable career and reprised the role again for Hammer in 1970 with *Taste the Blood of Dracula*. This was followed by *Scars of Dracula* (1970), *Dracula AD 1972* (1972) and *The Satanic Rites of Dracula* (1974). Interestingly, in 1970, Lee also appeared in *Count Dracula*, a film that was not made by Hammer studios but was directed by Jesus Franco. The film claimed to be a more accurate adaptation of Stoker's novel and Lee follows the novel's physical descriptions of the count more closely. He begins the film as a grey-haired aristocrat closer to Stoker's vision and appears to grow younger during the film. Although the film also boasted Klaus Kinski in the role of Renfield and Herbert Lom as Dracula's nemesis Van Helsing, it has a poor critical reputation.

Blacula

Perhaps one of the most bizarre and unexpected reinterpretations of the Dracula story is the 1972 blaxploitation horror film *Blacula*. Although at the time of its initial release *Blacula* was an obscure and little-seen film, it has developed a reputation in the intervening years as a cult horror classic. The film was directed by William Crain and starred William Marshall as the lead character. The story begins in 1780 with an African ruler called Prince Mamuwalde looking for help from the unlikely figure of Count Dracula in helping him to fight the slave trade. As the epitome of evil in many people's minds, it is interesting to note that, in *Blacula*, the count is a racist. He rejects the pleas of Prince Mamuwalde and also vampirises him. Dracula then seals him in a coffin and dubs him with the racially insulting title of Blacula.

The film then moves forward in time to the then contemporary date of 1972 when the coffin that contains Blacula is shipped to Los Angeles. It emerges that it has been brought by a pair of gay interior decorators who unwittingly open the coffin and release the vampire. Mamuwalde stalks the city claiming new victims but falls in love with a woman called Tina whom he believes to be the reincarnation of his own wife. The odd nature of the murders that are taking place in the city soon leads the police to investigate the matter and they conclude that a vampire is at large. The film ends with Mamuwalde and Tina on the run from the police and she is shot during the pursuit. Mamuwalde, in a strange reversal of natural processes, saves her from death by making her into a vampire but she is finally tracked down by the police and killed with a strike through her heart.

This proves too much for the central character who is heartbroken at her loss and his final act in the film is to emerge deliberately from a subway tunnel into the daylight and destroy himself. He disintegrates grotesquely in the rays of the sun, bringing his reign of terror to an end.

Or so it seemed. Miraculously, the character of Blacula was raised from the dead by a voodoo priest for the wonderfully titled 1973 sequel *Scream Blacula Scream*. Although *Blacula* was not a mainstream success it did perform well financially and sparked a slew of films that mixed horror with the style of blaxploitation movies. Other examples of this peculiar hybrid genre are *Blackenstein* (1973) and *Dr Black and Mr Hyde* (1976).

The Legend of the 7 Golden Vampires

Another example of the Dracula story being absorbed into a different and seemingly unlikely genre is the cult classic *The Legend of the 7 Golden Vampires*. This film was also released in different territories under the titles *The Seven Brothers Meet Dracula* and *Dracula and The Seven Golden Vampires*. Released in 1974, it was a co-production between Hammer Films and Shaw Studios, a film production company based in Hong Kong. As Hammer's fortunes were beginning to fail at this time, they attempted to breathe new life into the vampire film by combining it with the then current boom in martial arts cinema made popular by, amongst others, the legendary Bruce Lee.

The film was jointly directed by Roy Ward Baker and Chang Cheh who had worked on a number of martial arts action films in the past. However, upon its release, the film credits named only Baker as director. *The Legend of the 7 Golden* Vampires sees Peter Cushing reprising his role as Van Helsing with John Forbes-Robertson starring as Count Dracula. The scene is set during a lecture given by Van Helsing at Chungking University, formerly known as Chongqing, on the subject of vampires in Chinese mythology. He mentions in particular a small rural Chinese village that has suffered from vampirism for a long time whose location is unknown. However, after the lecture is finished, Van Helsing is approached by a student played by David Chiang who is seeking his assistance in ridding his village of vampires. Van Helsing agrees to help and he sets out to destroy the vampiric threat to the village along with his companions who include his own son and the student and his brothers. Van Helsing discovers that Count Dracula is controlling seven vampires who wear gold masks and are deadly martial artists. Although remembered for featuring some terrible dialogue *The Legend of the 7 Golden Vampires* has some impressive martial arts sequences and some bizarre and memorable imagery deriving from the influence of both Eastern and Western cultures. The film is also the last Hammer horror film that Peter Cushing was to make.

Chapter Eight

The Modern Cult of the Vampire

During the latter part of the twentieth century, the influence of *Dracula*, mainly through the medium of film, contributed to the creation of a kind of vampire subculture that has grown in popularity right up till the present day. Cinema has been the key vehicle for this but books and popular television series such as *Interview with the Vampire*, the *Blade* series and *Buffy the Vampire Slayer* have also helped maintain the iconic profile of Stoker's character. The interest in fictional vampires that can be found in a range of popular culture has at times spilled over into real life with claims that actual vampires exist, hidden within society.

The Highgate Vampire

One of the most bizarre and well-known claims of the presence of a real life vampire in recent years involves the case of the so-called Highgate Vampire. The story of the Highgate Vampire is of particular relevance here because it is a phenomenon that has clearly been influenced by Bram Stoker's *Dracula*.

The alleged mystery began in the late 1960s when a group under the name of the British Occult Society began spending time in the famous Highgate Cemetery at night. During these night-time forays into the cemetery the leader of the society, David Farrant, had what he believed to be a supernatural experience. He wrote a letter to the *Hampstead and Highgate Express* on 6 February 1970 in which he claimed that on 21 December 1969 he had spent the night in Highgate Cemetery and had seen a strange, tall figure with staring, hypnotic eyes.

He invited other local residents to report any strange occurrences that they had experienced in an attempt to identify the figure. It was reported in the paper on 13 February that other people also knew of a mysterious, tall man in a hat who had been seen in the cemetery or in the nearby area of Swains Lane that runs next to it. Others claimed that a phantom cyclist had chased women down the lane, unexplained voices had been heard, the sound of bells had emanated from a disused cemetery chapel and there had been other unusual sightings.

The story took a further twist when claims were made by Sean Manchester who lived locally that he was aware of the strange graveyard presence. He wrote to the *Hampstead and Highgate Express* on 27 February, stating that he had seen the corpses of foxes that had been mysteriously drained of their blood. He went on to say that a 'King Vampire from Wallachia', who had been a practitioner of black magic in the medieval period, had been transported in a coffin to England during the eighteenth century. He also said that the followers of the 'King Vampire' had secured a house for him in the West End of London. Manchester claimed that the Wallachian nobleman had later been buried in the ground that had become Highgate Cemetery and that modern Satanists had revived him. However, bizarre though the claims may have been, Manchester caused a greater controversy when he observed that people in the past would have dealt with the problem by staking, beheading and burning the unwanted vampire but, in modern times, such behaviour would be illegal.

Seizing on the lurid nature of the story the *Hampstead and Highgate Express* published it under the sensationalist headline of 'Does a Wampyr Walk in Highgate?'

In the same newspaper, David Farrant was reported

to have said that he had also seen dead foxes within the cemetery that appeared to have been drained of their blood. The interest in the story grew to the extent that, on Friday 13 March, both Farrant and Manchester were interviewed by ITV within Highgate Cemetery itself. Manchester said that he was intending to hunt for the vampire and it became clear that there was rivalry between him and Farrant. ITV also interviewed a number of other witnesses who claimed to have seen strange phenomena in the cemetery. After the series of interviews was broadcast Highgate Cemetery was beset by crowds of so-called vampire hunters, eager to find and destroy the alleged monster. Police drove them back out of the cemetery with some considerable difficulty.

Sean Manchester was to later claim in his book, *The Highgate Vampire*, published in 1985, that he and a number of others had entered the cemetery that night without police noticing. They made their way to a tomb which had been singled out to him by a psychic, sleepwalking girl. He attempted to open the door of the tomb but was unable to. However, according to his own account, he was able to find a way in with his companions through the roof and clambered down a rope to find empty coffins inside. They then put garlic into the coffins and holy water. The next development in the story of the Highgate Vampire was the discovery of the headless and burnt remains of a female corpse close to the tomb that Manchester had claimed he entered. Not long after Manchester was stopped outside the cemetery by police who found him carrying a wooden stake and a crucifix but a court case against him came to nothing. Both Farrant and Manchester were to claim that they had investigated the cemetery and carried out exorcisms.

As both men continued in their activities the tension between them grew and Manchester eventually challenged Farrant to a magician's duel that was to take place on Parliament Hill on Friday 13 April 1973. However, the paranormal showdown never took place and Farrant was sent to jail in 1974 for the desecration of memorials in Highgate Cemetery. He was to insist that the damage was carried out by Satanists and that he played no part in it. The enmity between Farrant and Manchester was to persist and both continued to write on the subject of the Highgate Vampire. The story of the Highgate Cemetery has remained popular partly because it has appeared in a number of books on ghost lore. Manchester also went on to found an Apostolic Church of the Holy Grail and has become its bishop. The influence of *Dracula* is evident in many of the details of the story: the

European nobleman carried to London in a coffin; a sleepwalking girl who mirrors Mina Harker; and a tall mysterious figure with the appearance of burning eyes. Both alleged paranormalists also clearly viewed themselves as fulfilling the role of Professor Van Helsing.

Francis Ford Coppola

Probably the best-known film adaptation of *Dracula* in recent years is the version directed by Francis Ford Coppola. The director appeared to be making his intentions clear by calling the film *Bram Stoker's Dracula* (1992) but critics observed that it deviated from Stoker's original novel in a number of ways. Coppola's adaptation of the novel is, however, closer in spirit to Stoker's story in that it makes the link between the fictional character of the vampiric count and the real life figure of Vlad Tepes from whom Stoker drew inspiration and whose name he used for his tale. The film begins in 1462, with a prologue not found in the book, and Gary Oldman playing the part of Vlad the Impaler. Faced with a Turkish attack on his home country of Wallachia, Vlad successfully defeats the Turkish army and the film depicts in silhouette impaled victims he has had set along the roadside. However, whilst Oldman's character has been away at war, his wife Elizabeta played by Winona Ryder has been falsely informed that he has been killed in battle. Heartbroken, she commits suicide by flinging herself from the window of the castle. Upon his return Vlad is told by an orthodox priest that his wife will be eternally damned for her actions at which point he explodes with rage and attacks the cross in the chapel of his castle, renounces God and swears vengeance, saying that he will rise from the grave after his own death.

The film resumes in the late nineteenth century and follows the narrative of Stoker's original as the young estate agent Jonathan Harker, played by Keanu Reeves, travels to Count Dracula's castle in Transylvania to finalise the sale to Dracula of Carfax Abbey, a property in London. Dracula's appearance at this point in the film is that of a strange white-haired old man who is dressed in long, trailing, blood-red garments. Harker is unnerved by the bizarre nature of Dracula and his castle, much as in the original novel. However, a crucial difference between this film version and the novel is that, upon seeing a cameo picture of Harker's fiancée Mina (Winona Ryder again) Dracula believes that she is the reincarnation of his wife Elizabeta who killed herself at the beginning of the film.

Jonathan Harker remains trapped at Dracula's Castle, weakened and terrorised by the three 'Brides of Dracula' who drink his blood and enfeeble him. Dracula himself sets sail for England aboard the *Demeter* and is finally carried to London in one of the boxes containing Transylvanian soil. Upon his arrival in London, Dracula vampirises Lucy Westenra, played by Sadie Frost. As in Stoker's original, the count grows younger through drinking the blood of his victims and is transformed into a dandyish heartthrob who follows Mina through London's Piccadilly area. He introduces himself to her and, through drinking absinthe, she is able to remember their shared past. Meanwhile Van Helsing recognises that Lucy is becoming a vampire and Jonathan Harker is finally able to escape from his imprisonment at Castle Dracula. He writes to Mina and the two plan to marry. Lucy is attacked by Dracula again and becomes his 'creature', changing finally into the form of a vampire.

Following her death and burial, Van Helsing and his fellow vampire hunters confront the vampiric Lucy and dispatch her with a stake through her heart.

Harker (who has been prematurely aged by his ordeal) and Mina marry and are enlisted in hunting the count. After his refuge of earth-filled boxes is destroyed Dracula appears to Mina and tells his story and she drinks blood from a wound in his chest. They are discovered and Dracula is driven away, fleeing England by ship, but he is now connected to Mina through their vampiric act. Van Helsing and his helpers pursue Dracula after Van Helsing hypnotises Mina to find out Dracula's plans. She and Van Helsing arrive at the castle before the count but she is rapidly becoming a vampire and has to be prevented, by means of a piece of Holy Communion wafer, from attacking the Professor. Van Helsing destroys the 'Brides of Dracula' the next day with stakes through their hearts. The other members of the group pursuing Dracula arrive, chasing the carriage of the count which is protected by gypsies. The two groups fight one another but, as the sun sinks beneath the horizon, Dracula emerges from his box of earth. Harker takes revenge against the count by cutting his throat whilst Quincey Morris thrusts his bowie knife into his heart. In an ending very different to that of the original novel, Mina drives off the hunters and accompanies Dracula into the castle's chapel.

He begins to age and asks that Mina allow him to die and, as they kiss, the candles in the chapel where he renounced God reignite. He appears to be forgiven for his crimes and Mina gives him the final rest he asks for by plunging the knife into his heart and cutting off his head. The film proved to be a huge popular and commercial success all around the world. It has, in fact, become the most financially successful of any of the many adaptations of Bram Stoker's novel. Interestingly, the film was shot entirely on sound stages rather than on location and in this sense has something in common with the 1931 Universal adaptation of the novel.

It is interesting to note that many of the novel's themes seem to have particular relevance to modern filmmakers and their audiences. In a review for *Variety* magazine from 9 November 1992 Todd McCarthy observed that: 'Coppola doesn't push it, but underlying everything here, as perhaps it must with any serious vampire story today, is an AIDS subtext involving sex, infected blood and the plague.' (Ronald Bergan, *Francis Coppola: The Making of his Movies*, p.138).

Shadow of the Vampire

In *Shadow of the Vampire* (2000), directed by Elias Merhige and produced by Nicholas Cage, the focus is on the filming of *Nosferatu* by FW Murnau in 1922.

The plot of *Shadow of the Vampire* revolves around the idea that the actor Max Schreck, who is playing the frightening count, is, in fact, a real vampire. The other actors on the film set believe that Schreck, played by Willem Dafoe, is an incredible method actor who never drops character. The film reveals that Murnau, played by John Malkovich, has made a deal with this real-life vampire that he can bite the neck of the film's leading lady in exchange for the most convincing portrayal of Dracula ever filmed. Willem Dafoe turns in a fantastically compelling performance of the undead count and was nominated for an Oscar as Best Supporting Actor. The film also received an Oscar nomination for Best Make Up.

Dafoe's performance is of particular interest because, in many ways, his vampire conforms more closely to folkloric descriptions of Nosferatu as animalistic and repellent rather than suave and attractive. The film also has a strong element of black comedy with Eddie Izzard as the hapless estate agent lured to the count's castle, here renamed Hutter rather than Harker, and John Malkovich often hilarious as the maniacal auteur that puts his art before all other considerations. It could be argued that the focus of this version of the Dracula story is on using it as a vehicle to explore metaphorically the vampiric nature of the medium of cinema. In a key conversation between film director Murnau and his leading lady Greta, arising from her frustration that she will not be able to act in the theatre because she will be away on location filming *Nosferatu*, this theme is made explicit.

Murnau: 'Why would you possibly want to act in a play when you can act in a film?'

Greta: 'A theatrical audience gives me life, while this thing (gesturing to the film camera) merely takes it from me'.

Prophetically, the train that takes the crew away from Berlin to film on location at the abandoned monastery where the count lives, in Czechoslovakia rather than Transylvania, is named *Charon*. In Greek mythology, Charon is the name of the ferryman who rows the dead across a river or lake to the gates of the Underworld where the terrible god Hades ruled. Murnau uses local people in filming *Nosferatu* who are genuinely afraid of vampires. When the director removes the crosses from the wall of a country inn a local woman bursts in on the director and crew while they are filming a scene to protest about their actions. Malkovich is hilarious as the emotionally detached but obsessive Murnau screaming to the producer, 'A native has wandered into my frame!'

It soon becomes apparent that there is something very strange about Max Schreck as he begins to prey on the cast and crew, much to Murnau's frustration and irritation. The film shows sympathy for the plight of the vampire who, in some ways, shares the characteristics of a drug addict, trapped in a narrow world of repetitive behaviour and driven by one compulsion only. *Shadow of the Vampire* also makes a number of blackly comic points about the profession of acting and what is necessary to turn in a convincing performance. Murnau dryly informs his leading actress whom he intends to sacrifice to the vampire, 'It is a very difficult role. It is a role that will make you great as an actress. Consider it a sacrifice for your art.'

The film climaxes with the vampire attacking Greta for real in its final scene and killing the other crew members whilst Murnau continues to film in the midst of the madness. Ultimately, Murnau outwits the count and destroys him by exposing him to sunlight just as in the original film *Nosferatu*. Interestingly, the count's death is visualised as a frame of melting celluloid, thereby intertwining the metaphor of the vampire with the medium of filmmaking.

Kim Newman

One of the most interesting and perhaps underrated re-imaginings of the Dracula character in recent years has been Kim Newman's unorthodox take on Bram Stoker's creation. Newman is well known as an author, journalist and broadcaster and has become closely linked with the vampire and horror genres through his series of books featuring the count. In his 1993 novel *Anno Dracula*, Newman offered an entirely different ending to Bram Stoker's story where Dracula manages to defeat Van Helsing and his group of vampire slayers and fulfils his stated intention to conquer Britain.

In Newman's bizarre and amusing take on the theme of what he describes as a 'Dracula Wins' outcome, the count, having survived the efforts of Van Helsing's group, goes on to replace Prince Albert and become the consort of Queen Victoria.

British history becomes entirely altered as Newman interweaves other characters from literary history into his plot such as Dr Polidori's Byron-inspired Lord Ruthven who becomes Prime Minister.

According to Newman, he first became fascinated by the character of Dracula after his parents let him stay up late when he was 11 years old to watch the

1931 film of *Dracula* starring Bela Lugosi. On the Kim Newman website where he gives the background to his idea for *Anno Dracula* the author notes that, 'I was captivated by *Dracula*, and became an obsessive in the way only an 11-year-old can be obsessive. I think my parents expected the craze to wear off, but obviously it never did'. Interestingly, whilst studying at university in 1978, Newman completed a course called Late Victorian Revolt which was taught by the poet Laurence Lerner and Norman MacKenzie who was the biographer of the legendary science fiction author HG Wells. As part of this course Newman wrote a thesis entitled *The Secular Apocalypse: The End of the World in Turn of the Century Fictions*.

Newman identified a number of novels and short stories from this period that feature a concern with an imagined outcome where Britain has been overwhelmed by an enemy power or force. Examples included *The War in the Air* (1908) by Wells and George Chesney's *The Battle of Dorking* (1871). Newman noted that many of these obscure science fiction tales from the past with their alternative views of British history could be considered the progenitors of later twentieth century stories in which the Nazis win the Second World War. He also quirkily observed that the character of Count Dracula in Bram Stoker's novel could be argued to represent a 'one-man invasion'. For Newman the main underlying theme of *Dracula* is Bram Stoker's fears about the fragility of the Victorian family and its values. The battle waged between Dracula and Van Helsing is essentially an attack on Victorian values that must be thwarted and, in Stoker's novel, Dracula is not allowed to succeed. A key quote from Stoker's novel to which Newman draws attention is Van Helsing's observation that Dracula intends to be, 'the father or furtherer of a new order of beings, whose road must lead through Death, not Life.' (Bram Stoker, *Dracula*, Penguin Classics, p322).

Having created this new alternative history of England, Newman then hinged the plot of *Anno Dracula* on the horrific real-life events surrounding the murders of Jack the Ripper. In a number of horror stories, including Robert Bloch's 'Yours Truly Jack the Ripper' (1943), the Ripper has been portrayed as a vampire, but in Newman's topsy-turvy world, where vampires are in power, he becomes a vampire killer. His identity is also taken from *Dracula* as Dr Jack Seward, driven over the edge by the staking of his beloved Lucy Westenra, enacts a terrible campaign of violence against vampire prostitutes in London's East End. The conceit of incorporating the Jack the Ripper story line also allowed Newman to move the action in *Anno Dracula* throughout the imagined Victorian Gothic London that he had created from the slums of the East End to the corridors of power stalked by vampires.

Some have argued that the events described in Bram Stoker's original novel took place in 1893 because the dates he gives fit that year. *Dracula* was, of course, originally printed in 1897 and its closing chapter describes events that took place seven years previously. However, interestingly Newman, along with the Hammer film version of *Dracula*, places his storyline in 1885.

Newman has followed an imaginary timeline into the twentieth century with a sequel to *Anno Dracula* called *The Bloody Red Baron* (1995). In this story the events of the first book lead into the First World War because, of course, vampires have the advantage over mortals in leading excessively long lives. The third novel in Newman's vampire trilogy is *Dracula Cha Cha Cha* (1998) set in Rome during the 1950s. Even more recently, the celebrated comics writer, Alan Moore, employed a similar approach in his *League of Extraordinary Gentlemen* stories which also plunder Victorian genre fiction and have narratives based on it. Moore notably borrows the character of Mina Harker from Bram Stoker's novel and has her join the eccentric and strange band of alternative superheroes upon which the stories are based.

The Historian

Interest in the Dracula legend has been reignited in recent years by the bestselling novel *The Historian* by Elizabeth Kostova. Published in 2005, *The Historian* caused something of a sensation in the publishing world when a bidding war for the rights to the novel resulted in Kostova receiving an advance of £1.1m. This was a large amount by any standards but was particularly unusual because it was her debut novel. The advance appears to have been merited because, on its first day of release, *The Historian* sold more copies than Dan Brown's *The Da Vinci Code* (2003) had on its first day. In some ways it is an unusual book to have become a bestseller. It is over 600 pages in length, quite intricately structured and based on a great deal of careful, measured research. The basic plotline of the novel is that Count Dracula, or more specifically his real life counterpart Vlad the Impaler upon whom Bram Stoker based the original character, was really a vampire and has survived into modern times.

Kostova spent ten years working on the book and much of its content draws upon her own experiences. The novel begins with the teenage daughter of an

American diplomat, working in Amsterdam, who discovers a strange, ancient book in her father's library. When she approaches him about the mysterious book, which contains only blank pages apart from two pages at its centre with a medieval woodcut of a dragon holding a banner displaying the word *Drakulya*, he reveals his quest to find the burial site of Vlad the Impaler. In an interview about the novel Kostova said, 'When I was a little girl, my father, a professor, took his young family to Eastern Europe on a fellowship. We travelled in Eastern and Western Europe, and along the way he amused me with a series of pleasantly creepy tales about Dracula. His stories were based on the classic Dracula films he'd grown up on. I loved these stories, and because of them Dracula has always been associated for me with travel and with beautiful places in the Old World.' (Interview with Mark Flanagan at About.com, Contemporary Literature).

Kostova believes that there are particular factors that have led to the success of *The Historian* and other historical thrillers such as *The Da Vinci Code* in recent years.

'We have experienced intense globalisation in the last 10 years and we are aware as never before of history as a whole and of our place in it....I also think this is an age of great anxiety. The more I studied the Middle

Ages the more I thought we hadn't come that far in some ways.' (Interview with Gary Younge, guardian. co.uk, Monday 18 July 2005).

Dacre Stoker

The cult of Dracula and the interest in vampirism show no signs of diminishing and indeed there is a sense that events have come full circle as the great-grand-nephew of Bram Stoker has published a sequel of sorts to the original novel.

Dracula: The Undead was written by Dacre Stoker and horror screenwriter Ian Holt and published in the UK on 24 September 2009. *The Undead* was of course the title that Stoker had originally planned for *Dracula* but was rejected by him at the last minute. Prior to its publication there was enormous interest in the book and the publishing rights were sold to an alliance of Dutton US, Harper UK and Penguin Canada for a figure said to be one million dollars. It was the first story to receive the full backing of the Stoker Estate since the 1931 film adaptation of *Dracula* starring Bela Lugosi. The authors describe the book on its official website as 'a bone-chilling sequel based on Bram Stoker's own handwritten notes for characters and plot threads excised from the original edition'.

It is set 25 years after the ending of the original novel and the authors follow the story of the surviving characters. Jonathan Harker, tortured by Mina Harker's remaining link to Dracula, has become an alcoholic. Dr Jack Seward, also deeply affected by the events of *Dracula*, is now a morphine addict and obsessive vampire hunter. Arthur Holmwood is no happier, trapped in a miserable marriage. Quincey Harker, the son of Jonathan and Mina, leaves law school for the London stage where he encounters Bram Stoker himself who is involved in a production of *Dracula* at the Lyceum Theatre. The play is a troubled affair which the author is producing and directing himself. Quincey Harker learns about his parents' real experiences with Dracula and it soon appears that the story is far from closed. In a tangled plot that overturns much of what the original novel describes, it transpires that the original reason for Dracula travelling to London was to combat the evil vampire Elizabeth Báthory who was the figure behind the Jack the Ripper killings. Not only is Dracula, it turns out, both noble and principled but it emerges that he is, in fact, the father of Quincey Harker.

The novel drew mixed reviews following its

publication. Noted *Dracula* scholar Leslie S Klinger wrote in his review of the novel for the *Los Angeles Times* of 25 October 2009, that *Dracula: The Undead* was not really a sequel to the original because 'no author would permit a sequel that boldly claims the original got the story wrong'. Klinger goes on to point out that the authors have included much material based on the lives and legends of Vlad the Impaler and Elizabeth Báthory as well as the horror convention, invented by the 1922 film *Nosferatu*, that vampires can be killed by sunlight. These influences, Klinger argues, go beyond the scope of the original novel itself. He also points out that they 'have fiddled with history', particularly contesting the claim that Bram Stoker continued to manage the Lyceum Theatre after Sir Henry Irving's time. However, he concludes that *Dracula: The Undead*, 'is a fine book in its own right, one that pushes the story in unexpected directions while remaining true to the dark heart of the Transylvanian vampire-king'. Dacre Stoker also produced a prequel to *Dracula* in 2018 called *Dracul*.

Today the ongoing influence of Dracula appears to be more pronounced than ever as the subject of vampirism has shown a surge in popularity in novels, films, television programmes and popular culture in general. Mainstream blockbusters like *Van*

Helsing (2004) and *Underworld* (2003) have proved particularly popular with young audiences. One of the most interesting films to feature vampires in recent years was *Let The Right One In* (2008), based on the Swedish novel of the same name by John Ajvide Lindqvist published in 2004. This Swedish language film drew widespread critical acclaim and was adapted into an English language version in 2010 under the title *Let Me In*. Focusing on the relationship between a bullied young boy called Oskar and a centuries-old vampire who takes the form of a young girl called Eli, the film echoes the increasing trend for stories that show sympathy for the plight of the vampire. Indeed, the metaphor of the vampire in many current fictions appears to be one of personal alienation and isolation in modern society. The book and the Swedish language film of the same name take their title from the Morrissey song *Let The Right One Slip In* from the 1988 album *Viva Hate*. Another notable popular success in the vampire film genre has been the *Twilight Saga*, again drawn from an existing series of books by the author Stephenie Meyer. Beginning with *Twilight* (2008) the series explores a relationship between a teenage girl, Bella Swan, and a handsome young man who is also a vampire called Edward Cullen. The role of

Cullen was played by the actor Robert Pattinson who has become a huge heartthrob to fans of the series. The success of the film led to a second instalment with *Twilight Saga: New Moon* (2009) and *Twilight Saga: Eclipse* (2010).

Mark Gatiss and Steven Moffat

Probably the best-known adaptation of Bram Stoker's novel *Dracula* in recent times is the BBC television series written by Mark Gatiss and Steven Moffat. This highly idiosyncratic and imaginative take on Stoker's story took the form of three episodes that premiered on BBC1 on 1 January 2020 and continued over the following two nights. Both writers had previously worked together on the television series *Sherlock* which began in 2010, based on Sir Arthur Conan Doyle's famous detective, and also the relaunched and reinvigorated *Doctor Who*, so they were no strangers to working with iconic characters.

The first instalment of the series, entitled *Rules of the Beast*, begins in a convent where a man whose face is disfigured is being interviewed by Sister Agatha Van Helsing about recent traumatic events he has experienced. The disfigured man is revealed to be

Jonathan Harker and he relates how he travelled to Transylvania to stay at the castle of Count Dracula and assist him with a property purchase in London.

Upon his arrival at the castle Harker is met by Count Dracula who is, at this point, an elderly man. Harker finds himself a prisoner in the castle and the count begins to feed on his blood. He becomes increasingly enfeebled whilst Dracula transforms into the handsome and more youthful form of the Danish actor Claes Bang. As Harker becomes more desperate to escape, he searches the castle and discovers in its labyrinthine corridors the count's other undead victims. Dracula refers to his victims as his brides and, in a roof top confrontation, kills Harker. However, Harker has now become one of the undead himself and, desperate to escape, hurls himself from the roof of the castle into the river that runs at its base. He is carried out to sea where he is discovered by a fisherman and then taken to the convent where he began his tale at the start of the episode. Sister Agatha Van Helsing is accompanied during her questioning of Harker by another nun. She is revealed to be his fiancée Mina whom he no longer remembers.

In a veiled reference to the television series *Sherlock*, which Mark Gatiss and Steven Moffat had previously worked on, Sister Agatha tells Harker, 'Having established your identity, it was not difficult to trace you back to England and find your worried fiancée. I have a detective acquaintance in London'. Horrified by what he has become and terrified that he will attack his fiancée, Harker tries to kill himself with a stake. Meanwhile Dracula arrives at the gates of the convent in the form of a wolf, drawn by the presence of the young Englishman. However, we learn from Sister Agatha Van Helsing that the count cannot enter the convent without being invited inside. Dracula then crawls up the walls of the convent to the room where Harker is staying. He reveals the information that the undead cannot kill themselves but offers to end his existence in return for being invited inside. In his desperation, Harker agrees to the offer and, once inside, Dracula slaughters all of the nuns and traps Mina and Sister Agatha in a lower level of the convent. Sister Agatha offers her life to Dracula but threatens to kill herself if Dracula does not let Mina go. Dracula accepts but makes the sinister promise to Sister Agatha that he will 'make her last'.

In the next episode, *Blood Vessel*, Dracula embarks on his journey to England aboard a ship travelling from the port of Varna called the *Demeter*. The ship contains a diverse selection of passengers as well as carrying boxes of Transylvanian soil.

It emerges that the *Demeter* was chartered by an unknown figure called Balaur whom nobody aboard the ship has ever seen or spoken to. Once the ship is on its way Dracula begins to kill the passengers and we learn that, in this version of vampiric lore, he acquires the abilities, memories and characteristics of his victims. It transpires that Dracula is Balaur and that he is purposely preying on these individuals amongst the crew and passengers as a means of preparing to arrive in Victorian England.

Amongst the passengers are a Lord and Lady Ruthven, a clear reference to the classic vampire story, *The Vampyre* by John Polidori, published in 1819. The survivors on board the *Demeter* search for the killer and finally break into cabin number 9, a berth which has previously been kept off limits to crew and passengers by the ship's captain. The mysterious cabin number 9 marks another insider reference by writers Mark Gatiss and Steven Moffat, this time to the television series *Inside No. 9* which first aired in 2014. This acclaimed horror-comedy show is written by and stars Steve Pemberton and Reece Shearsmith with whom Mark Gatiss had previously worked on *The League of Gentlemen* comedy television series. The survivors on the *Demeter* discover the occupant of the cabin is Sister Agatha Van Helsing who appears seriously ill and close to death. Dracula has been feeding on her blood but tries to convince the crew and passengers that she is, in fact, the killer amongst them. Throughout this episode Sister Agatha has been hallucinating that she has been playing a game of chess with Dracula in which he describes the voyage to her. When she asks him why he chose to travel with others he replies, 'I like people'. Sister Agatha then poses the question, 'Then why do you kill them?'. Dracula wryly answers, 'Why do you pick flowers?'.

However, despite the count's attempt to blame her for the murders on board, Sister Agatha is able to persuade the others that Dracula is the real perpetrator.

Following a struggle, the survivors are able to set fire to Dracula and he leaps into the sea to escape them. However, their relief is short-lived as he reappears when the *Demeter* is close to Whitby and it emerges that he survived his ordeal by fire, and got back on board the boat and concealed himself. In a final bid to destroy the vampire before the ship makes landfall, the captain blows up the vessel with gunpowder as Sister Agatha keeps the count talking. Once again Dracula survives the attack and, swimming underwater, finds one of the boxes filled with Transylvanian soil on the seabed and climbs inside it. After an indeterminate period of time Dracula leaves his coffin and walks ashore underwater to Whitby where he emerges on the beach at night. But his victory in reaching England is short-lived as he is immediately discovered and detained by the modern-day Jonathan Harker Foundation.

In the final instalment, *The Dark Compass*, broadcast on 3 January 2020, the episode begins in daylight on the beach at Whitby 123 years on from the events aboard the *Demeter*. Dracula has escaped from the Jonathan Harker Foundation and has found a victim in Whitby and is hiding inside their home. He marvels at the modern inventions that they contain whilst also recognising how mundane their setting and uses have become. Dracula observes, 'I knew the future would bring wonders, I did not know it would make them ordinary'. Having fed on modern victims Dracula is able to 'download memories' through their blood. He is then recaptured by the Jonathan Harker Foundation led by Dr Zoe Helsing, a descendant of Sister Agatha who keeps him in a laboratory in order to study him. During this recapture Dracula bites Zoe but her blood makes him sick and weakens him because she is suffering from cancer. They are not able to hold him long as he contacts a lawyer called Frank Renfield played by Mark Gatiss who is able to free him from the control of the Foundation. Meanwhile Zoe Helsing drinks a sample of Dracula's blood in order to understand him and is able to share the memories of her forbear Sister Agatha Van Helsing. Once freed, Dracula enters modern British society and falls for a beautiful, nihilistic and narcissistic young woman called Lucy Westenra who has no fear of death. Dracula drinks her blood and makes her his latest bride. Dr Zoe Helsing travels to Dracula's home to attempt to destroy him with Lucy's ex-boyfriend Jack Seward who is also involved with the Jonathan Harker Foundation.

Lucy Westenra is now one of the undead and she also arrives at Dracula's home, unaware of the horrific changes that have taken place in her appearance. When she realises that she is no longer the beauty she once was she pleads with Jack Seward to kill her. He agrees and drives a stake through her heart. In an echo of the first Hammer production of *Dracula,* Dr Zoe Helsing attempts to destroy Dracula by exposing him to direct sunlight, leaping from a table to pull down the curtains over the windows as Peter Cushing did when playing the role of Van Helsing. However, Dracula is unaffected by this and Zoe explains to him that all of his supposed weaknesses to the symbol of the cross and sunlight are in fact manifestations of his fear of death. Although he is from a long line of warriors who died courageously in battle, he is forced to admit that he is, in fact, a coward. He is shown as a wretched and tortured individual in many ways, although he is also callous, cruel and indifferent to the suffering of others. In this television adaptation, he is depicted as acting very much like a modern-day serial killer in that he exhibits violent psychopathic criminal behaviour. Moved by what Zoe has said to him, Dracula decides to end his own life by drinking Zoe's blood and the cancer that it contains. Zoe tells him that, 'the blood of the dying is death to the vampire'. Finally, the two warring enemies die together, finding some kind of peace at last, bathed in sunlight.

The Dark Compass was followed later in the evening by a documentary by Mark Gatiss entitled *In Search of Dracula*. After researching the origins of Stoker's character and the author's working methods, Gatiss explored the development of Dracula in film and television. The documentary also revealed that some of the filming for the 2020 BBC television series had taken place at Orava Castle in Slovakia. FW Murnau's 1922 film *Nosferatu* had previously used the same castle as the setting for Count Orlok's home in Transylvania. Similarly following in the tradition, other scenes from the television series had been shot at Bray Studios in Berkshire where Hammer Film Productions had made many films including the 1958 *Dracula*, (1958) with

Christopher Lee in the starring role. Gatiss ended the programme by concluding that Dracula can be seen as 'evil's own hero' and observed that it is unusual for such an evil character in fiction to be so famous.

Critics generally received the series extremely favourably. Lucy Mangan, writing for *The Guardian*, described the first episode as, 'a bloodstained love letter to a classic, beautifully and delicately scented with just the faintest hint of ham gothic yarns need...' and concluded that *Dracula* was 'a blood-sucking delight that leaves you thirsty for more.' (*The Guardian* website, Wed 1 Jan 2020). However, Keith Watson, writing for the *Metro* newspaper, was less positive saying that, 'the first part of this three-part character study felt naggingly like style over substance' and described it as a 'fitfully entertaining misfire'. (*Metro* Website, Wed 1 Jan 2020). For Claes Bang, taking on the role of Dracula was both an exciting and daunting prospect. Speaking in an interview with fellow Danish actor Sofie Gråbøl, Bang commented that, '...before we started shooting, I was terrified, because it is very iconic. He's got his own emoji!'. (*Radio Times*, 21 December 2019-3 January 2020, p55).

Despite the iconic status of the vampire count, writers Mark Gatiss and Steven Moffat were clearly unafraid to radically reinterpret Bram Stoker's original story and character. Arguably, this modern, darkly funny and unconventional version of *Dracula*, which featured a strong female character at its centre as well as gay and black characters, actually continued a long-running pattern in the history of cinematic and televisual adaptations in reflecting the concerns and values of the writers and societies that produced them. For example, the vanity of Lucy Westenra's character can be seen as Gatiss and Moffat taking a swipe at the current 'selfie generation' of Instagram users and, more broadly, a comment on the youth-obsessed nature of modern society and its reluctance to face the grim reality of mortality. This version of *Dracula* also restored some of the fear and horror which the original novel and some film adaptations succeeded in provoking in audiences but which time and cliché have to some extent lessened. As actor Claes Bang noted, Dracula now has his own emoji and spin-offs like the Count von Count from Sesame Street have made the character perhaps rather too cuddly and familiar. Roxy Simons, writing for the *Daily Mail* website on 1 January 2020, reported that, 'viewers are left terrified by first episode of *Dracula* with its decapitated nun and bloodthirsty babies'. In the same article one twitter user was quoted as saying, 'How the hell am I supposed to sleep tonight@BBCOne? #Dracula was terrifying but brilliant. I will keep a light on for sure'.

Bram Stoker's own original story tapped into the fears of its times and can be seen as sharing some of the concerns of the then popular literary genre known as Invasion Literature, as discussed earlier in this chapter. This form of fiction became popular in the United Kingdom between 1871 and the outbreak of the First World War (1914-1918). The genre was first launched with the publication of the novella *The Battle of Dorking: Reminiscences of a Volunteer* by George Tomkyns Chesney in 1871. It describes the military invasion of Britain by a German-speaking power, a concern that spoke to the real anxieties and paranoias of the British during this period. *Dracula* arguably represents a supernatural variation on this theme in which Britain is threatened by a sinister foreign force landing at the port of Whitby.

It is interesting to note that the 2020 television adaptation of *Dracula* by Mark Gatiss and Steven Moffat was produced at a time when fears around the dangers of unchecked immigration from Europe had resulted in the Brexit political movement and the UK's departure from the European Union. Whether either writer, consciously or unconsciously, considered this social anxiety is debatable but nevertheless it demonstrates the ongoing potency of the Dracula story in its ability to mirror social fears through the ages. However, it seems clear that the predominating themes shared by many modern vampire fictions and Stoker's original novel are those of sex and death. The basic human concerns of the fear of mortality and the primal sexual urge transcend time and setting and therefore have universal relevance. Modern audiences continue to be thrilled and disturbed by the theme of vampirism in much the same way as Victorian audiences were by Stoker's novel although clearly the subject also has a large degree of symbolic flexibility. It may have been an act of unwitting genius on the part of Stoker that he created a story and a character that harnessed these powerful and often subconscious fears and urges and have proved not only to be enduring, but also ever-evolving. The figure of Dracula looks set to continue to both attract and repulse audiences well into the future and Stoker's novel has undoubtedly achieved an enduring immortality of its own.

Bibliography

Bibliography

The Holy Bible, New Revised Standard Version, Oxford: Oxford University Press, 1995

Auerbach, Nina & Skal, David, *Dracula*, New York: Norton, 1997

Baker, Roy Ward, *The Director's Cut*, London: Reynolds & Hearn Ltd, 2000

Bergan, Ronald, *Francis Coppola: The Making of His Movies*, London: Orion, 1998

Chessex, Jacques, *The Vampire of Ropraz*, London: Bitter Lemon Press, 2008

Copper, Basil, *The Werewolf: In Legend, Fact & Art*, London: Robert Hale, 1977

Farmer, David, *Oxford Dictionary of Saints*, Oxford: Oxford University Press, 2004

Florescu, Radu R & McNally, Raymond T, *Dracula, Prince of Many Faces: His Life and Times*, New York: Back Bay Books, 1989

Frayling, Christopher, *Nightmare: The Birth of Horror*, London: BBC Books, 1996

Gelder, Ken (ed), *The Horror Reader*, London: Routledge, 2000

Graves, Robert, *The Greek Myths: Combined Edition*, London: Penguin, 1992

Holroyd, Michael, *A Strange Eventful History*, London: Chatto & Windus, 2008

Jones, Alan, *The Rough Guide to Horror Movies*, London: Penguin, 2005

Jones, Stephen, *Clive Barker's A-Z of Horror*, London: BBC Books, 1997

Leatherdale, Clive, *Dracula: The Novel & The Legend*, Desert Island Books, 1985

Lee, Christopher, *Lord of Misrule: The Autobiography of Christopher Lee*, London: Orion, 2003

Rigby, Jonathan, *English Gothic: A Century of Horror Cinema*, London: Reynolds & Hearn Ltd, 2004

Shelley, Mary, *Frankenstein Or The Modern Prometheus*, London: Penguin, 2003

Stoker, Bram, *Dracula*, Oxford: Oxford University Press, 1998

Stoker, Bram, *Dracula*, London: Penguin, 2003

Stoker, Bram, *Dracula*, London: Penguin Classics, 2011

Stoker, Bram (edited by Byron, Glennis), *Dracula*, Peterborough, Canada: Broadview Press, 1997

Stoker, Bram (edited by Leslie S. Klinger), *The New*

BIBLIOGRAPHY

Annotated Dracula, New York: Norton, 2008

Stoker, Bram, *Dracula's Guest and Other Weird Stories*, London: Penguin, 2006

Trow, MJ, *Vlad the Impaler: In Search of the Real Dracula*, Stroud: Sutton Publishing, 2006

Westwood, Jennifer and Simpson, Jacqueline, *The Lore of the Land*, London: Penguin, 2005

Index

Also By Giles Morgan

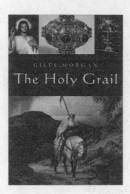

The Holy Grail is a subject that fascinates and intrigues. Through its various guises as magic cauldron, cornucopia, horn of plenty and chalice cup it has remained at the centre of popular culture from antiquity right up to the present day. An object of marvel and mystery it inhabits a place in mythology that has its roots in historical facts.

9781904048343   9.99

St George is a figure that bridges many worlds. At the heart of the myths and legends surrounding this English icon lies the story of an Early Christian Martyr persecuted by the Roman Empire. England is only one country to have adopted this legendary soldier saint as their patron, others include Germany, Armenia, Hungary, Portugal and Malta. The cult of St George is astonishingly widespread with churches being dedicated to him in Ethiopia, Egypt, Greece and France.

9781843449652   6.99

The Byzantine Empire is now recognised as having had a considerable influence on the Renaissance and a significant impact in the shaping modern Europe and modern historians are increasingly acknowledging the role the Byzantine Empire played in the development of both Islam and Christianity. The Byzantine Empire lasted for over a thousand years, created remarkable art and architecture and a lasting cultural and religious legacy – even its decline and fall was to have ramifications that reached far beyond its borders.

9781843445951   8.99

The world of Freemasonry exerts a powerful influence on the modern imagination. In an age when perceived notions of history are being increasingly questioned and re-examined it is perhaps inevitable that secretive societies such as the Freemasons find themselves at the centre of considerable speculation and conjecture. To some they represent a powerful and shadowy elite who have manipulated world history throughout the ages, whilst to others they are an altogether more mundane and benign fraternal organisation. Giles Morgan explores the obscure and uncertain origins of Freemasonry.

9781842438886   8.99

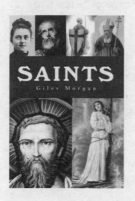

For millions of people saints provide comfort, hope and inspiration and act as intercessors to God. But whilst the earliest saints and martyrs served an essentially spiritual role within society their impact and influence can also be found today throughout the modern secular world. The term saint comes from the Latin word 'sanctus' meaning Holy. Many of the first saints were Christian martyrs who died for their faith. The original meaning of the accolade of martyr was 'witness'.

9781843449706   3.99 (ebook)

A Short History of the Anglo-Saxons traces the fascinating history of this era and its people, from the early migration of European tribal groups such as the Angles, Saxons and Jutes who mainly travelled to Britain after the end of Roman rule in 410, to the dramatic end of the Anglo-Saxon period following the victory of William the Conqueror at the Battle of Hastings in 1066. This short history explores the kingdoms of Wessex and Mercia, Alfred the Great's defence of his realm from the Vikings and the final Norman Conquest. Also included are the compelling discoveries of Anglo-Saxon relics in modern times and many other gems.

9780857301666   9.99

○LDCASTLE BOOKS

POSSIBLY THE UK'S SMALLEST
INDEPENDENT PUBLISHING GROUP

Oldcastle Books is an independent publishing company formed in 1985 dedicated to providing an eclectic range of titles with a nod to the popular culture of the day.

Imprints vary from the award winning crime fiction list, NO EXIT PRESS, to lists about the film industry, KAMERA BOOKS & CREATIVE ESSENTIALS. We have dabbled in the classics, with PULP! THE CLASSICS, taken a punt on gambling books with HIGH STAKES, provided in-depth overviews with POCKET ESSENTIALS and covered a wide range in the eponymous OLDCASTLE BOOKS list. Most recently we have welcomed two new digital first sister imprints with THE CRIME & MYSTERY CLUB and VERVE, home to great, original, page-turning fiction.

oldcastlebooks.com

OLDCASTLE BOOKS	KAMERA BOOKS	HIGHSTAKES PUBLISHING
POCKET ESSENTIALS	CREATIVE ESSENTIALS	THE CRIME & MYSTERY CLUB
NO EXIT PRESS	PULP! THE CLASSICS	VERVE BOOKS